VET ON CALL

Tim looked on in astonishment. He had delivered calves in the veterinary hospital and in barns and byres, but he'd never delivered a calf on a ledge perched precariously above a three metre drop onto hard ground. Calves wriggled; and if the cow slipped, down would come cradle and baby and all.

He shook himself awake.

'It strikes me I'd be better learning mountain rescue than veterinary medicine,' Tim said, as the farmer and Tamsin steadied the ladder. He climbed three rungs and slipped. . .

Fresh out of college, Timothy Yorke soon discovers that theory and practice don't always work together!

VET ON CALL

Joyce Stranger

CAROUSEL BOOKS
TRANSWORLD PUBLISHERS LTD.

VET ON CALL
A CAROUSEL BOOK 0 552 52131 0

First published in Great Britain by Carousel
Books Ltd.

PRINTING HISTORY
Carousel edition published 1981
Carousel edition reprinted 1981

Carousel Books are published by
Transworld Publishers Ltd.,
Century House, 61-63 Uxbridge Road,
Ealing, London, W5 5SA.

Made and printed in United States of
America
by Arcata Graphics
Buffalo, New York

Dedicated to
Ann and Ellis
with appreciation

Chapter 1.

Tim pulled out his battered old suitcase from the cupboard in the fireplace wall, and blew the dust off it. He was leaving in the afternoon, saying goodbye without any regret at all to the farm where he'd been working for the last four months.

He had needed the money, or he would never have stayed. It was nothing like any farm he'd known before. The stink from the pig styes was everywhere; he wondered if it would ever wash off. He put the suitcase on the bed and looked at the initials. His mother had given him the case for his eighteenth birthday, the year he started at college.

It seemed like a lifetime ago.

Goodness knows why she'd had to put all his initials on.

T.I.N.Y.

Timothy Ivan Neil Yorke. Now M.R.C.V.S. too. Member of the Royal College of Veterinary Surgeons. At last.

Why couldn't they have called him Neil Ivan Timothy; but that wouldn't do either. N.I.T.Y. Timothy Yorke would have been better. Timothy was his father's choice; with Ivan for his mother's father and Neil for his father's father.

He supposed that, after having three girls, his parents had been so pleased with a boy that they'd had to land him with all the family names. It meant that he went through life called Tiny by almost everyone; and as he topped 1.8 metres, with broad shoulders and fists that packed a pretty hard punch in the school and college boxing rings, he sometimes felt he could've had a much better name. He had spent his school life trying to live his nickname down, by pretending to be much tougher than he was.

He shoved his fingers through his mane of dark auburn hair, and glanced over his shabby surroundings. The bed was lumpy and not yet made. The room itself held nothing but a battered chair, a chest of drawers and a rickety wardrobe that threatened his life every time he went near it. The farm was at the back of Nowhere, with a view across bleak moors, where scrawny sheep grazed. He'd wanted more experience with pigs; and they had pigs. Oh yes, they had pigs all right!

The door slammed open.

'Going to work today or not?' George was three years younger than Tim. He disliked Tim and had never troubled to hide the fact. He resented everything about him; his height and his six years at college most of all. George was short and dark and chunky. He looked at the case and grinned.

'Going to put M.R.C.V.S. on that too?' he asked. 'Tell the world about it?'

'I'm coming', Tim said, determined not to start a row on his last day. Soon he would never see George again; it was a thought to cherish.

'I've done the milking. Thought you weren't bothering to do 'owt today. I've left you Pearly, George said, and went off in the direction of the pig styes.

Thank you very much for nothing, Tim said to himself. He was never going to see Pearly again either and he wished wholeheartedly that he wasn't going to see her today.

Pearly was just about the oldest Shire horse in existence; it was rumoured that she was fifty, but horses didn't live that long. Whatever else old age had done for her, it had made her awkward and cunning. Go in with her water and she shuffled round the stable and stood on your foot; bend over and a well aimed hoof sent you flying into the manger; try to groom her and her teeth took hold of your hair and pulled, or dug into the lobe of your ear. Put your hand in her manger and you were lucky to come out with all your fingers.

Taking her out of the stable into the field was an exercise guaranteed to reduce strong men to tears, as she dug in her hooves and insisted she was too old to go outside; she was too tired to go outside; it was too wet; or it was too sunny; or it was too windy; or she just didn't feel like it today, thank you.

But no-one could clean her stable out while she was in it and no-one could leave her standing in her own muck for the day, so out she had to come.

It took argument; it took tugging; it took pushing; it took pleading; it always took ten times as long as anyone had, and it reduced everyone to fury and Joel Thomas, who owned the farm, to a state of gibbering rage.

He would watch Tim struggle; he would watch George struggle. His eyebrows rose into his thatch of uncombed hair; his jaws worked, but no words came and when everything else has failed he exploded.

'The good Lord give me patience! Can't anyone manage a horse round here? Coom oop, then me pearly beauty,' and out came Pearly, her ears flicking round to listen, in case either George or Tim had something to say, and stepped gently and easily, without fuss or bother, into the field. She hung her head over the gate and positively crooned when her master scratched behind her ears.

'Can't think what I pay you for,' the old man grumbled, every single day, without fail. It was the only time that George and Tim ever agreed. The old horse had the devil in her.

Today was no different.

Pearly leaned against the stable door, making it

impossible for Tim to open it. Her head weighed like a sack of potatoes. He tried to push her back and she grabbed his hair. He should've been ready for that! He was not going to lose his temper, not today. He was a fully fledged veterinary surgeon with a string of letters after his name to prove it. He had passed, contrary to his and his father's expectations.

He was going to have a week at home and then he was off for his new job. And however much he'd hated life on the farm, this had been a good preparation for it, because the new village was out in the wilds too. It was a huge practice covering a great many kilometres. A country area, just what he'd wanted.

He wasn't quite sure that his new employer was exactly what he wanted though. He was an old man by Tim's standards and would have no truck with new fangled ideas; he'd said so at the interview. Tim was full of modern ideas.

That was in the future. What lay now in the present was getting Pearly out of her stable and into the yard, and then cleaning out the muck. She seemed to have had too much to eat the day before and rejected most of it; he had hours of work ahead and he'd hoped to finish early.

George passed him, on his way to the pigs, and grinned evilly. He'd tried to get Pearly out of her stable earlier, but she was in one of her worst moods. Mr. Clever M.R.C.V.S. Tiny Yorke could struggle on his last day. He hoped Pearly would kick Tiny – or stand on his foot. Him and his degree; some people had all the luck and didn't deserve it.

Tim struggling with Pearly, returned some evil thoughts about George. George hadn't had to work like a slave for six years, sweating over books, getting knowledge the hard way. He didn't have to satisfy any examiners. George didn't give him any credit for his hard work – though maybe George would have to stay on this farm for the rest of his life and that certainly would be penance enough.

'Out you come, girl,' Tim said, aware that Joel Thomas was stamping across the yard, his face dark with anger. Now what had gone wrong? Was it just indigestion or his wife not getting breakfast ready early enough? Come to think of it, Tim hadn't had any breakfast and felt he could eat Pearly's rations he was so hungry. But there would be no food till this job was done.

Joel leaned against the stable wall, puffing smoke from his extremely unpleasant old pipe across Tim's face. Pearly hated smoke. She reared and came down with a forehoof on Tim's foot. Tim, tears in his eyes and gasping for breath through pain, wondered if his foot was broken. It would be a fine way to start a new job.

'Dear Mr. Fitzpatrick, I'm sorry that I can't come. A horse broke my foot.'

Very competent.

'All them letters after yer name don't seem to have taught you much,' Joel observed.

Tim lost his temper. This great lump of a horse was coming out today if it was the last thing he ever did. She wasn't going to play silly games with him.

She'd bitten his fingers, pulled his ear, tugged at his ear, butted him in the chest, pushed against him, leaned on him and shoved him down into the filthy muck of the yard which was never cleaned up properly and across which twenty cows marched every day, leaving plenty of evidence of their passing.

Somewhere behind him a litter of small pigs were screaming like demented creatures as George came down the line of styes with the swill. A cow was bellowing mournfully, announcing that she was going to calve in the evening, or during the night, and she'd make the most of the occasion.

Tim's foot was on fire. He would never walk again. He would get gangrene and it would have to be amputated and he'd be the only one legged vet in history who was crippled before he'd even had time to start his career.

The horse was coming out of the stable and he'd wipe that look off Joel's face for ever.

Temper tautened his resolve. Today he would be master and my lady could lump it!

'You are coming OUT!' he said, and took the rope attached to her halter, and, without even contemplating the idea that she would disobey, led the way outside.

Pearly knew a lot about people. She'd learned over the years who was afraid of her and who she could bully. She knew she dared never try her tricks on Joel. He had a calm authority that told her that she might suffer for them; how she was never sure, as she'd never had the chance to find out. It was always better to do as Joel said, at once. Every beast on the farm knew that.

Oddly, Joel had never harmed any of them. He simply understood animals, an understanding that went deep into his bones; and though his farm was rundown and his beasts in poor condition, he could handle any creature, even a half mad bull, as he had no fear whatever and every confidence in himself. On the other hand, he could never understand people. They were too complicated and Joel was a simple man.

Tim had been wary of the old horse; George loathed her and was terrified of her; and she knew that about both of them. The smell of fear was unmistakable; an acrid smell that irritated the horse beyond measure, so that she reacted nastily and at once.

Tim's pain and fury had banished his wariness. He was no longer afraid of her but he still didn't like her. Today, he suddenly didn't care. She would come out or else. He wasn't quite sure what 'or else' would be; it was difficult to think of ways of arguing with a mountainous black Shire mare, but he had no intention of letting her get the better of him and she reacted to his mood.

Meekly she followed him out into the yard. He tethered her to the ring on the wall that had once been a tethering ring for bulls.

Joel dropped his pipe.

'So them letters did do you some good,' he said caustically. He turned away, sorry to have missed the chance of putting Tim in his place once again. Too sure of themselves by half, these lads.

Tim decided to ignore Joel's sarcasm. Instead he pitched quantities of soiled straw into the big barrow, working doubly hard, determined to finish and leave early. Working on Pearly, he thought with longing of Bracken, the first pony he had ever known. Bracken had belonged to Uncle Sam, who bred Welsh ponies. She was part Arab, was kind, was gentle, and followed him everywhere like a dog. He had haunted Uncle Sam's stables, had learned to ride on Bracken, and knew far more about horses than any other animals. It was Uncle Sam who'd persuaded him to become a vet.

'Far too few good horse vets,' he was fond of saying.

Tim wondered just what Uncle Sam would've made of Pearly. Uncle Sam had died a year ago. He had left Tim a vast library of books on horses. Tim missed him. He had known so much – but he'd never owned a horse like Pearly.

Joel looked at Tim's back and stamped over to the styes to goad young George, who was fending off twelve small piglets who seemed determined to eat him as well as the swill. One of them was in the trough, being shoved by his brothers and sisters. Behind them the sow grunted as she tackled her own food, gobbling and swallowing with the noise of ten sows. Old Gert was the greediest animal even Joel had ever known and he'd known plenty of pigs. He liked pigs but they could be very awkward.

Half a pig himself, George thought, as the old man leaned over the stye and scratched Gert's broad back. She paused and eyed him and returned to the trough.

It was lunch time before Tim was through. He put clean straw down in the stable, brought in a bucket of water to stand and let the chill off it, and walked Pearly round the yard for her daily exercise. The fields were too swampy to use. It had rained for days, a never ending misery that turned the cow field into a morass and the yard into a slippery trap that sent you flying if you were not careful; and lying in that was mucky to say the least.

'Your last day,' Bess Thomas said. 'I've made summat special. You leaving after lunch?'

Tim nodded. He liked Bess. She was a plump small woman who was endlessly busy and who coped with Joel's tempers as she coped with the animals; with gentle endurance.

'Have trouble with Pearly?' Bess asked, knowing the answer.

'She came out like a lamb,' Tim said, grinning as he remembered. It was one of the few things that had happened in the whole four months that he would remember with pleasure.

'That was a turn up,' Bess said. 'Pity it took you till today to learn how to manage her. She's an awkward old girl, but she's got nice ways for those she likes.'

And some pretty nasty ones for the rest of us, Tim thought. He looked at the table. An enormous casserole of meat and vegetables and herb dumplings which he loved; a mass of mashed potatoes and carrots; and an apple pie with the thick clotted cream that Bess made every night, putting the pans on the stove to separate while they slept. The big Aga was kept in day and night, summer and winter, making the kitchen into a hothouse where Bess grew three windowsills full of plants that rampaged all down the wall.

Unlike the yard, the kitchen was immaculate and boots had to be left in the porch. Tim walked in his socks across to the sink to wash, and paused as he heard a small mew from under the table.

'Has Snowy had her kits?' he asked, drying his hands.

'She's had two; reckon there's a third there, but she's having a bit of trouble with it,' Bess said. 'Maybe you could have a look at her?'

Tim crawled under the table. He wondered how other vets managed; did they end up in the undignified places he found himself in or was life composed only of surgeries and operating rooms and everything done as it was in a human hospital? Only the week before one of the other cats had had her kittens under the porch roof, and they'd rolled down under the eaves so she yelled till everyone was awake as she couldn't reach them. Tim had stood on a ladder in the dark, feeling for the tiny mites, and handing them down to Bess, while the mother cat alternated by purring at him as he foraged, and scratching him in an attempt to get her babies off him.

Snowy looked up at him. Two tiny replicas of herself were cuddled against her. She was struggling with a third which had jammed. Tim eased it into the world, and gave it to the cat to mother. If all his jobs were that simple. . . He grinned down at her. There was nothing quite so satisfying as watching an animal that had just given birth safely.

'Save us money, that will,' Bess observed placidly, putting a huge heap of food in front of him. 'I'd have had to get the vet out if you hadn't been here.'

I am a vet, Tim thought, with sudden surprise, but he didn't say it. He felt a small warm glow of pride as Snowy left her basket and rubbed against him. He scratched behind her ears and her noisy purr made Bess laugh.

'Not make much money if you do all your jobs free,' George said, grinning at him, prepared to be civil now that Tim was going. He ate fiercely, stuffing in the food as if the world would end before he finished and he intended to die well fed.

Back in his room, Tim emptied the clothes from the chest of drawers. He had left some in the suitcase, which was still on the bed, unopened. He unfastened the snap-lock, and noticed a hole in the end of the case. It was only cheap fibre, but even so there shouldn't have been a hole like that.

He opened the lid and stared.

There, in the middle of his underwear, in a nest made neatly of chewed-up paper from his college notes, was a small field mouse, four babies nursing from her. She glared up at him, her small nose twitching in fright. She had stolen food from Pearly's manger; a neat little pile of uneaten grain mixture lay just outside the nest. She must've worked for days, but he couldn't leave her there. He picked up the nest gently and looked warily round before he went outside.

They'd think him mental if they saw him carrying a mouse nest neatly built in a pair of brightly striped underpants, towards the barn. She was obviously a field mouse come in for shelter. The cats would probably get her, but at least he was giving her a chance. He tucked the nest well out of sight at the back of the hay and went back to his room to shake out his clothes and pack the rest of his belongings. He wouldn't be sorry to leave the place; he hadn't enjoyed himself at all. It had been an unusually cold and early autumn, with several frosts, and his room reminded him of the cold store in a butcher's. It was nearly as cosy.

He thumped the bed and the worn out springs protested. No more noisy nights. He wondered suddenly if his new home would be as bad. Nothing could be as bad – could it?

He looked at peeling wallpaper and the damp patch

on the ceiling that looked like a bull's head; at the old wardrobe and the rickety chest; at the rag rug by his bed and the bare wooden boards.

He hoped the mice would enjoy the peace; he heard them at night, racing round the wainscoting as if they wore skates; scrabble, scutter, scratch and squeak. He had spent most nights hoping they were mice and not rats. There were certainly rats in the hay. The cats caught them and so did Snarler, who was quite the most evil Jack Russell he'd ever met, ready to sink his teeth into everyone except Joel and Bess. These he loved devotedly and with misapplied heroism as on occasion he decided that innocent people meant harm and needed attacking.

Joel often told the story of the Government Inspector who had marched in without a by your leave, and run off with Snarler hanging from his trousers, teeth sunk in firmly, refusing to let go.

'Better guard than any Alsatian,' Joel said.

Snarler and Tim had had a wary truce. You leave me alone and I won't touch you. The dog watched him now, as he made his way across the mucky yard to the barn where his car waited.

It was a twelve year old, blunt nosed, somewhat decrepit Morris Minor, both side doors carefully stencilled with the words *San Francisco Fire Department*, which had amused him at the time but now seemed rather silly. He would have to do something about that before arriving at his new job.

He would have to buy some decent clothes, too. His wardrobe of jeans and old jerseys, and the US marine jacket with its insignia intact, wasn't going to get him much respect from clients. Nor was the antique duffle coat with only one toggle, and one shoulder eaten by a goat that he hadn't noticed when he left it over a wall on his last day at college, when they had gone out to a farm to see a cow with an unusual growth on her shoulder.

'You're off then,' Joel said, as Tim stooped to get inside the kitchen door. He did remember this time not to straighten up until he was between the black beams. 'Want your money, I suppose?'

Tim couldn't imagine anyone not wanting their wages.

Joel was counting five pound notes.

'Have to send you the rest; I'm short this week; had a lot of expenses and forgot you were going,' Joel said.

It had been the same every week. Tim had almost lost count of what he was owed as their transactions became more and more involved; the three pounds I owed you from the week before last and the ten pounds from last week. That makes us four pounds short this week which I'll give you next week; only next week when he got the four pounds Joel owed him, Joel was five pounds short again. Somewhere, Tim was sure, he was the loser on all this as somehow, however he wrote it down, it never added up right.

'Eight pounds I owe you. I'll put a cheque in the post,' Joel said.

Tim doubted it very much but there was nothing he could do about it. He said goodbye and went outside.

'So yer off,' said George.

Tim nodded.

The last thing Tim heard as he swung out into the lane was the squeal of the little pigs, yelling for more food. He was sure that the noise they made broke all the limits of the Noise Abatement Act, but how did you stop piglets yelling? The screams died away as he moved out into the lane, the engine, as usual, misfiring. Not long now, and he'd have a new car of his own as part of his job; and a flat of his own.

He'd be working with animals, curing them but not mucking them out any more. No more piglets to be fed, or nipping him as he bent down to fill the troughs. No more struggling to give a piglet a bottle; no more fights with Pearly in the morning; no more mucking out the stables.

He'd have a job of his own; and money of his own; and a life of his own. He couldn't wait to begin.

Chapter 2.

Tim enjoyed being home for exactly two days. He looked up old friends, sorted out the books he needed for his new job, turned out his college notes, keeping those that would be useful, marvelling at some of the things he'd had to learn. He wondered how many of them would come in handy, or if he would end up like his mother's brother, a busy G.P., who complained bitterly that if he saw anything unusual after years of measles and mumps and chickenpox, coughs and colds and cut fingers, he wouldn't even recognise it.

He glanced through his notes. Oddly, dogs and cats were fairly strange to him. He had kept an owl, bred rabbits, tamed a hawk and farmed stick insects, which were a pest as they ate privet and all their own hedges were beech. He'd gone round the district pinching privet leaves, filling his pockets. They weren't even likeable – he couldn't imagine why he'd ever kept them, except they didn't make a mess. His mother hated mess.

New Forest Disease: this affected the eyes and could cause blindness. . .

So did a number of other things; and did it matter really what they were called if the animal still went blind in the end? Though maybe if you knew how blindness could occur, you might be able to prevent it in the first place. You certainly could when blindness was carried through breeding. Tim knew more than most people about breeding – dogs, anyway – though he didn't know nearly enough. His mother's sister, Aunt Dora, bred poodles. Not the tiny poodles that most people knew, but the big standard poodles. She gave him long lectures on the evils of picking the wrong sire or the wrong dam; of avoiding dogs that carried blindness and could pass it on to their puppies; of watching for good hips, and above all of making sure the animals had good temperaments and were nice to be with, as savage dogs, timid dogs, frightened dogs and wicked dogs, all tended to pass on their behaviour to their young.

He had spent more time though at Uncle Sam's stables. He'd always longed for a horse of his own, but it was much too difficult to own one. He pretended Bracken was really his and had been desperately unhappy when she died of old age. No pony would ever quite replace Bracken. On the other hand, he'd had little to do with dogs. Uncle Sam had no time for them at all. Grandfather always kept a couple of sheepdogs, but they were working dogs, living outside and never allowed indoors, or to be petted. They had to earn their keep.

Like father like son was a true enough saying, but grandparents were even more important in ancestry. Tim's grandfather had been a hill farmer, and Tim had inherited much of his love for animals from him. He would even have liked to farm himself, but grandfather died leaving nothing behind to carry on the place, which had to be sold; so there was no money for farming in his family. You needed money to start, even in a small way; money for buildings, to buy animals, to buy food for them; and it cost a fortune to feed a horse properly; and Tim would've liked to breed horses. Racehorses. Elegant beauties with Arab blood; the best horses in the world.

By the third day at home he was beginning to feel bored. His friends were all busy at their own jobs. Jock, who'd been his sparring partner at school, was now working in a bank; Sam, who might have come fishing, was busy in a factory. Hilary, who might have walked the hills with him, was a doctor's receptionist and Susie, his first love, had taken her pilot's licence and was working with a charter firm in Canada, leading a very exciting life.

Everybody was working except him. His father left early in the morning; his mother seemed to be moving him around the place all day, wanting to vacuum the floors, or dust the furniture, or make the beds, or turn out the cupboards, or clean the bath. By some stroke of genius he was always in the room she wanted to do next.

He took his car to pieces and put it together again; painted over the sign saying *San Francisco Fire Department*. It looked awfully bare without the words, but he was having a car provided when he got to his new job, and hoped to sell this one, if it would fetch anything. At least it still went.

He shopped for his mother. It rained continuously so he couldn't even tidy the garden, still burdened by the weeds of last summer, which had turned out wetter than any summer Tim could remember.

He shopped for clothes, buying a decent anorak, a couple of thick jerseys, and three respectable pairs of jeans, which were the most useful of all garments for messing about with cows and sheep and horses. His mother had knitted him two pullovers and given him shirts for his birthday – soberer shirts than he cared for. So he went out again and splashed out on two more in brilliant red and blue checks, and a heavy duffel coat for winter weather.

'Your Aunt Dora rang,' his mother said as he came in from this shopping expedition. 'She's got something for you, as a reward for passing your exams; and to help you in your new life.'

Aunt Dora was his mother's elder sister, but where his mother was small and dainty, Aunt Dora was more like her father's side of the family. She was a big untidy ungainly woman, her grey hair pulled back into a tight bun, or else flying loose over her face, giving her a witchlike look. She wore old clothes that she bought from the Good-As-New shop, saying clothes were a waste of money. Wellington boots, thick gamekeeper-style trousers, heavy, shapeless jerseys and coats that always seemed either a size too small or several sizes too large.

She lived in a tiny cottage at the end of a lane; one bedroom upstairs, a little sitting room, and a huge kitchen, whose main feature was an enormous counter built right along one wall, on which were stacked dog bowls and tins of dog food; packets of dog biscuits; packets of dog food; jars of vitamin tablets and garlic tablets and seaweed powder and various tablets guaranteed to give good coats, or get rid of show nerves, or give gleaming eyes; and right at the end was an enormous glass jar filled with bran and another with bonemeal.

Making up food for the dogs was a major occupation as each of her dogs had a different amount based on its body weight, so that the scribble pad at the end of the draining board was covered in calculations as to size of dog and food helping. Those that didn't thrive at all on her meticulous regime were given extras; potatoes and sponge cake made with butter; eggs and cream and custard; anything to put on weight. No vet would've approved of her diets.

Tim laughed, but no-one laughed at her successes. The staircase wall was covered in rosettes and prize-cards: red Firsts and blue Seconds predominated. She had bred three Champions and had a bitch that had been Best in Breed at Cruft's. Her present stud dog, a large brown dog named Colonel Groans, was her rising star, and already had a Junior Warrant.

That had been exciting as Tim had been on holiday at the time and Aunt Dora had asked him to help her with the dogs at the shows. They'd travelled widely, as Groby, which was her pet name for Colonel Groans, had only needed his last four points. He had to get twenty five points for the Warrant before he was eighteen months old, and now had only four weeks to go to get the final few.

Tim had been as anxious as Aunt Dora as they had sat poring over *Dog World* to find out what shows were on and where, in the little time they had left. The Open Shows only gave Groby one point if he won his class and got First Prize; it was the big Championship Shows they needed, where the judges awarded the coveted Challenge Certificates. Groby wasn't in that class yet and it would be a year or two before he could compete as he was still not much more than a puppy. But First Prize at a Championship Show meant three points, so if they could get one point at an Open Show and three at a Championship, Groby would be there.

It had been a cliff hanging, nail-biting experience. At the first show, all the way to Exeter for an Open, Groby had come second. No points at all. Then Crewe Open and one point. Then came two Championship Shows and the time was nearly up. Another three days after the second show and Groby would be too old.

They had gone to the first show and Groby had been beaten again. No points at all, although he'd been shown in two classes and come second in each. So nearly there.

Last time, Aunt Dora had said. She had dressed more carefully than usual and Groby looked wonderful. His coat was in perfect condition; eyes bright, he was totally eager, and even Tim, who would've preferred a German Shepherd to a standard poodle any day, had thought that today Groby ought to win. He looked absolutely gorgeous.

It was agony to watch the judge; the dogs lined up and waiting; the handlers moving them round the ring. Aunt Dora looking as if she was praying at every step.

There were twenty two in the class. A big class and a lot of competition. Tim watched, almost too excited to breathe, as the judge began to select the dogs. Groby stood like a hero. He was moved into third place, that wasn't good enough; into second place and Tim began to pray too, pray that the judge would move him up; they needed those three points and today was the last chance.

Someone stepped in front of Tim and he could've knocked the man down as he blocked his view. The ring-side watchers were clapping as Tim pushed forward – and there was Aunt Dora with her face threatening to split in two, being handed the red card.

She came out with it and hugged Tim.

'We've done it,' she said at the top of her very considerable voice. 'In the nick of time. . .'

It was time for Groby's next class and that, too, he won. So at the end of it all, they had more points than they needed and the coveted prize for a young dog; that Junior Warrant now framed an on the wall. One day perhaps three championship certificates would hang beside it; and he would have the most coveted title of all.

It had been a day Tim would remember all his life, even if he never went to another show.

He thought of it now as he drove to Aunt Dora's. He'd never been interested in showing before, but the excitement had got to him and he shared her triumph. They had stopped on the way home and had a terrific meal at a big hotel, dressed in their dog clothes and not caring at all, and Aunt Dora had lashed out on champagne, which he didn't even like, but drank to honour the occasion.

It was a grey day, with the sun trying to shine through the clouds, as he drove along winding lanes. A visit to Aunt Dora always turned into a riot – a welcome one after the oppressing boredom of the past few days. Dogs were in the garden and dogs were in the house; dogs were in the sheds and dogs were in the kennels; only none of them, ever, were exactly where they ought to be, so that Aunt Dora rushed round trying to find Colonel or Major, or Captain or the General, while Admiral was missing and Bosun had gone to ground under the wheelbarrow and the bitches were all in the wrong places too.

The dogs always had 'service' titles; the bitches had names that began with a Z. Aunt Dora never did things the easy way. She had named her kennels Zenophon; so her bitches were Zenophon Zeta and Zenophon Zebra, and Zenophon Ziggie. Tim regarded Ziggie with deep loathing, as she spent her life trying to love him to death, and launched herself at him, usually filthy and stinking, as she loved to roll in things that humans regard as unspeakable. Whatever he was wearing wasn't only ruined but stank for several days after that

'She does loves you so, dear,' his aunt said when he complained.

Aunt Dora's presents, like her dogs, weren't always what he wanted either. She had given him a most beautiful pale pearly pink hairbrush for his twelfth birthday, which would have been lovely for one of his sisters. Tim had done his best to lose it, without success as his mother regarded presents as sacred. You never gave them away and you took great care of them. The hairbrush had spent most of its recent life inside a wellington boot, as his mother, to his utter horror, had packed it with his college clothes. Luckily he'd been alone in his room when he unpacked. He thrust it deep into a disused wellington with a hole in it, and covered it with an unwashed sock, which ensured that no-one else ever looked inside.

Aunt Dora had also given him three copies of *Treasure Island* at various times, never remembering what she'd given the year before.

For all that, Aunt Dora's teas were memorable, so long as you waited until she'd fed the dogs and didn't mind the smell of dog or the muddle.

Almost there, past the Master and Maid, where the meals were beyond the price of the average diner; past Hanging Cross, down Gallows lane, and into his aunt's yard.

The dog-proof gate to the garden was almost people proof too. He fought it and slipped through. In the foreground playing tug with a large stick, were three poodle puppies. They forgot the stick and launched themselves at him instead, their small bodies hard against him as they hit his legs. He knelt to pet them, amused by their behaviour.

'Nothing wrong with those temperaments,' Aunt Dora said. It was one of her hair flying free days, and it seemed to have grown thicker and longer and woollier in the time that Tim had been away. Her brown cardigan hung on her, buttoned up the men's way, but buttoned wrongly, so that one side was much longer than the other. She appeared to have been wading in deep clay, as mud clung to her baggy trousers and large green wellington boots.

'I've just got Zero and Zuleika to feed,' Aunt Dora said. 'It's getting hard to think of Z names; do you know any nice diseases, dear, with names beginning with Z?'

'Offhand, I don't think there are any,' Tim said, pushing puppies off him, as he stepped over a large brown dog that seemed to regard the doorstep as the only place where he could lie; not making the slightest move to get off it.

'That's Brigadier,' Aunt Dora said. 'Nice, isn't he? He has a beautifully strong foreface; just what the judges look for. He's quite the laziest dog I've ever known.'

She led the way indoors.

'Isn't there one Z illness? There are four bitches in this

litter and I must have names for all of them; it's getting so difficult.' She glanced at her scribble pad. 'Puppy feeding time. It won't take a minute, dear. Tea's all ready in the sitting room and I remembered to shut the window so that Poohsey and Plop can't get in.'

Poohsey was a very large and remarkably smelly tomcat who well deserved his name; his tabby body was scarred all over, as he fought every other male in the area, and occasionally tried to fight the dogs. That Aunt Dora would not allow, and Poohsey was 'abolished' to the big shed outside where next door's tractor lived, and locked in. Poohsey was always being 'abolished'. Aunt Dora never could get words right, but Tim preferred her words to the proper ones – they sounded better.

Plop was a small fat ginger cat with a sweet face, and habits that were far from sweet. She ate mice and sicked them up on the table – PLOP! Tim thought he probably loathed Plop even more than he loathed Ziggie. Aunt Dora never had nice cats because hers mostly lived wild and lived outside, kept as ratters.

'Guess what Ziggie did?' his aunt said, as if she'd read his thoughts. She was mixing puppy milk with an antiquated egg whisk that squeaked as it whirred. She added two eggs to the mixture and went on whirring. 'I believe in raw eggs for coats, whatever they say; or you say. I suppose you're on their side now.'

Tim knew she was talking about vets; she had always had the idea that the veterinary profession was out to prevent her from carrying out her own ideas whenever possible, and that most of them knew nothing about dogs.

'What did Ziggie do?' Tim was watching the pups race around the yard, apparently convinced that they were greyhounds. They were the wrong shape at that age – roly poly and unformed, giving no hint of the adults they would become, and still unable to run very convincingly so that the result was endearingly absurd. Tim laughed as one fell over and whimpered, and his mother ran to him and licked his face. He sat, tugging at a teat.

'Had puppies?' Tim said, as the whirring stopped. It seemed a safe guess.

'No, dear. She fell in the septic tank. The men had come to inspect it and taken the lid off. It took me three hours to get her even half way fit to live with. I smothered her in eau-de-cologne in the end. Can you ask your mother to get me some more from Boots? It's so useful.'

With Ziggie, it was.

Aunt Dora had pushed her hair out of her eyes, found her reading glasses, which she'd left beside the boiler in the outhouse, and was once more doing calculations on her fingers.

'Puppy 1 needs more bonemeal than puppy 2. Tim, I MUST have names for them. Z names now, quick. What's the use of all those letters after your name if you can't even think of a few puppy names?'

'Can't you change to A or B, or C?' Tim asked. Z really was an impossible letter.

'No, dear. The boys all have rank; and it's useful too to have a trademark even if it is only in a name. Nobody would ever forget a name like Bossie Boots, the St. Bernard who won Cruft's, would they? If it's a dog from me, they always know it will be Zenophon Admiral or Zenophon Major, or Zenophon Captain; if it's a bitch it's a Z name. I can't change now. I've done it for too long.'

She began to measure the revolting looking mush she'd just produced in the mixing bowl into smaller bowls, each one marked with a number in black paint.

'It means the right puppy gets the right mixture,' she explained. She had a weird system all her own of working out feeds.

'I don't know how you tell them apart,' Tim said.

'Really, Tim. They're as different as Captain is from Ziggie. You must learn to use your eyes. You could make a name for yourself as a vet who is able to judge a good dog. Most vets don't know a mongrel from a pedigree and certainly can't tell a good well-made dog from one with fine bone and faulty coat and missing teeth. Well, they know missing teeth. Judges will put up with anything these days.' She pushed her hair back out of her eyes again. 'Now, what have I forgotten?'

Practically anything, Tim thought, hoping she didn't express such unfair and slanderous opinions about vets to all her friends. Knowing Aunt Dora, she almost certainly did. He started to think about Z names while she carried the bowls outside and squatted to call the puppies. Each pup was given its own bowl and she stayed beside them, making sure that all had their own food and no more from anyone else.

Feeding took very little time. The pups ate as if they'd never been fed before. His aunt was in with the bowls and scalding them from the kettle that always puffed steam on top of the huge Aga, almost before he had time to move. He could smell baking bread. Aunt Dora's bread tempted too many people to put on weight when they stayed with her; with goat butter that she made herself and honey from her own bees, no-one wanted any other food. The bread was thick and crusty and had a taste to it that few people knew in these days of factory loaves.

'Zinca; Zorilla; Zelia; Zoraya,' Tim suggested in desperation, knowing that if he didn't come up with something they would talk about nothing else all through tea.

'Darling, aren't you clever. Let me write them down. So those years in college did do some good after all. How did you think of them? Do they have meanings?' Aunt Dora was scribbling frantically.

'Zinca is just Zinc with an "a" added; a Zorilla is a sort of fox; Zelia is Celia with a Z; and Zoraya I think I invented,' Tim said.

'Well, when you have all that time to spare with no sick animals in your new job you can invent new names for me. Zeta's in whelp. Come and look at her and tell me if you think she looks well or not.' It was a ridiculous request, as even if Tim thought the bitch looked ill, his aunt would be indignant and refuse to believe him; she knew just as well as him whether her animals were fit or not.

Zeta was lying on her side in her pen looking extremely contented and placid. The pups were due in five weeks; she'd been mated four weeks before. She wagged her tail, but didn't bother to get up. She had much better things to do than to greet Tim; she and Tim tolerated one another. The one bitch he always did get on well with was Zippa, the mother of the little pups playing outside the kitchen door. One pup was sitting thinking, her head on one side; one investigating a smell, small nose very busy, and a third was being carried by Zippa back to the kennel where they slept, as she had decided they'd had enough exercise for one day and it was high time they went in.

'She always does that, every single day without fail, at the same time,' Aunt Dora said, as she stood the bowls to dry on top of the Aga. 'When she has them all in, I lock her up. She's a very good mother. I've sold three of the pups. I had to go to foreign names for the ranks; its getting very difficult to think up new ones even for the dogs. Do you think anyone would buy a puppy called Führer?'

Tim laughed.

'No, I don't, nor Dictator, or Tyrant. You could try President and Consul and Questor and Speaker and Chancellor.'

'You don't take life nearly seriously enough,' Aunt

Dora said. 'Never mind, I expect you feel hungry. My dogs always get ratty when they're hungry, too, and I have to watch fights don't break out.'

She led the way into the tiny sitting room, where Air Marshal, her retired champion, was stretched on the rug, the only dog allowed that privilege. He was twelve, and going deaf, but he stood to greet them and wagged his tail furiously as they came in.

'Who's mother's love?' Aunt Dora crooned.

Tim cringed inwardly. He hated people talking baby talk to dogs; they needed a firm friendly voice and to be treated with respect. Marshal was looking at Aunt Dora as if he agreed with Tim, but she had a piece of cake in her hand and he was willing to humour her.

'I made all your favourites,' Aunt Dora said, 'to celebrate. And we'll have some of my elderberry wine as well, after tea. We must drink a toast to your future. I'm sure you'll be a wonderful vet. When you're older, that is,' she added. 'No time for young men myself; need the corners rubbed off and to learn a little about life; full of lovely new theories, I expect, aren't you? Experience will soon show you that theories aren't always right.'

Tim was too busy eating to listen. He knew the lines the conversation would run on now; they were well travelled. Aunt Dora came to supper with his family about once a month and she and his father echoed one another's opinions.

She poured the tea into the glass beakers that she always preferred to china, and passed him a slice of chocolate cake filled with thick cream. If he visited many more people, and they all fed him like this, he would have to get back into training as soon as he started work or he'd be puffing like a grampus all day. Maybe he could take up boxing again; he might play rugger again too; he might do almost anything, if the practice wasn't too busy and he had enough time.

'You aren't listening to a word I'm saying,' Aunt Dora said.

'I'm sorry. The fire's so lovely and warm, it's making me sleepy,' said Tim, using an excuse that was, in fact, perfectly true.

'I was telling you about the show at Birmingham,' Aunt Dora said. Her voice was soothing, a background to eating, and Tim thought that one day he too would have a dog or dogs of his own, though he wasn't sure what breed. Certainly never a poodle. He wanted a sporting dog; a retriever perhaps, or maybe he would have a German Shepherd, a big handsome elegant dog.

'So come and see what I chose for you,' Aunt Dora said, breaking into his thoughts. 'I don't know if you're meeting a young lady after this, or what you're doing, but I might as well talk to myself for all the notice you're taking. I asked you twice if you wanted to see your present?'

'I'm whacked after that farm,' Tim said. 'They worked us like slaves.'

The remark was bound to get sympathy, and it did. His aunt promptly forgot that he hadn't been listening and talked about farmers who used sweated labour from young vets who hadn't passed their exams.

Tim had expected to be given a beautifully wrapped present, wrapped by his aunt's friend, Marilyn, who came three times a week to help with the dogs.

Instead, his aunt said to him, 'Go and stand by your car. I know you've had enough of me. Be off to your young lady.' Aunt Dora lived in a world of her own, Tim thought. And why on earth should he stand by his car?

'Turn your back,' Aunt Dora said.

This was getting idiotic, Tim thought, wondering if he ought also to hide his eyes. Maybe she'd forgotten he'd grown up. He couldn't imagine what she had in mind.

'Turn around,' Aunt Dora said.

She was carrying one of the puppies that had been playing in the yard. Tim supposed it had escaped, and she was on her way to put it back. He looked around to see if she'd put down a gift-wrapped parcel anywhere. If he saw the shape he might be able to guess and manage to sound fervently grateful.

'This is Zenophon Zia,' Aunt Dora said. 'What do you think of her?'

Tim looked at the pup. For a poodle, it was a nice poodle, but poodles weren't his favourite breed. He managed to say 'She's lovely,' in a voice he hoped was suitably enthusiastic.

'That's wonderful,' Aunt Dora said beaming all over her face. 'She's your graduation present; the foundation of your breeding stock; the pup in a million that's going to make you famous. I bred her just for you. I picked her just for you. She's a most intelligent little thing and she'll be great company when you get away on your own to your new job. You'll be so far away from us all, and you'll be so lonely.'

Aunt Dora made it sound as if he were going to Mongolia, or somewhere equally remote, instead of four hours away up the M1.

'I won't stay; take her home and settle her in, and here's her diet sheet, and here's her pedigree, and here's the transfer form for you to sign. Don't thank me, darling. I know you're overwhelmed, and you didn't expect anything like this. I don't often give away my puppies; I could have got £150 for her, so do treasure her. One thing, I won't have to worry over this one. I hate selling them. It's not so unselfish as it sounds as she'll be in the family which means that I can keep an eye on her, and you will mate her to the right dog, won't you? I'll tell you which dog to choose. Goodbye, my poppets,' she added, kissing Tim's chin and the puppy's head, almost in one movement and running indoors because she hated parting from the puppy.

He stood by the car looking down at the tiny animal that nestled in his arms.

The last thing he needed just as he started a new job was a nine-week old puppy, still having four meals a day; needing to be house-trained; needing all kinds of things that he wasn't going to have time for. He needed a new puppy like he needed a hole in the head. And he wanted a poodle puppy as much as he wanted to go back to the farm he'd just left.

Poodles were for old ladies and pretty women; not for vets. Though at least it was a standard poodle, and would grow into a big animal, not a tiny one. He wouldn't have it clipped, either; or show it, whatever his aunt said. He wasn't a poodle man and that was for sure.

What was also for sure was that he was stuck with it. He couldn't hurt Aunt Dora by giving it back; she'd probably never speak to him again, and he was very fond of her. His mother wouldn't keep it. It had been given to him and he would just have to take it to his new job.

Every family had an Aunt Dora, he supposed. Delightful, kind, and extremely unworldly. He sat in the car looking at the puppy and the puppy looked back at him. She was warm and furry and her small pink tongue came out and licked his hand. She was a pretty little creature, not yet too poodle-like. Her coat was a rich brown; her eyes looked up at him, as if weighing him up.

He had to learn to want her and like her. He had a dog now, and even though it was a breed he didn't want, a sex he didn't want, and given to him at a time that couldn't have been more inconvenient, he had to keep her.

Aunt Dora waved happily from her window, delighted to see Tim struck dumb, with what she thought was sheer delight.

He drove home with the pup lying quietly on the passenger seat beside him, surprisingly well behaved.

He drew up at the gate, and met his father, who'd just put his car away in the garage.

'What has Aunt Dora given you to help you on your career?' his father asked grinning, knowing very well that whatever it was, it would almost certainly be wildly unsuitable.

Tim lifted the puppy out of the car.

'A poodle bitch to start my own foundation kennel,' he said, and then, seeing his father's grin, stood and yelled with laughter. His mother, coming to the door, stood looking at the pair of the disapprovingly.

'Dora has just rung me, and it's a very kind thought,' she said. 'I don't know what the two of you are laughing at.'

Tim's father winked at him.

'Your mother would never understand,' he whispered.

Tim looked down at the brown furry bundle in his arms.

'Oh you, why in the world did she have to breed puppies like you?' he asked her, and Zia licked his hand, and curled against him, quite sure she was where she belonged.

Chapter 3.

Tim's mother was not fond of dogs which was why dogs had never been a major part of his life. The family had a cat, which Tim sometimes fed if no-one else was there to do so.

He had discovered in his car, a quantity of puppy-food, a large polythene bag filled with puppy milk powder, two bowls, one of which his aunt had labelled FOOD and the other WATER: a grooming brush, a comb, and a long lead that proved to be a lead and collar in one, with a slide on it to adjust it to the pup's neck.

There was also the diet sheet.

He put the pup down on the sitting room floor and looked at her. She looked back, squatted and produced a remarkably large puddle for such a small pup.

'Tim. Take her out to the kitchen at once. I can't imagine what your aunt was thinking about giving her to you today, while you still have three days at home. She knows how I feel about dogs. And just look at the carpet.'

Tim took the pup into the kitchen. He'd never house-trained a dog before; the cat had her own door and was clean from the start. He put Zia down on the floor, and found a cloth.

'Not that cloth; that's for cleaning the draining board. Honestly, Tim!' his mother said, snatching it from him, and going to the cupboard to produce a clean cloth, a bucket and cleaning fluid for the carpet.

He wasn't going to be popular at home. He was going to have a flat of his own; and how did he train a puppy by remote control, when he had to leave it alone all day? It would have to be with him in the car all day; he could surely work something out. If he cadged a big container from the grocers for it, so that it had a safe place to lie; and took its food with him; and stopped to exercise it every half hour or so. How long before it was old enough to understand? And had it been inoculated?

Oh, Aunt Dora, Tim thought. You do make life difficult. I can't put this present at the back of my wardrobe or in a wellington boot.

The pup was exploring busily. Tim, lost in thought, sat on the edge of the kitchen table absentmindedly helping himself to sausage rolls which his mother had put on a large dish. There seemed to be an enormous quantity of them. He wasn't even thinking as he ate; he must've eaten ten of them, as they were so tiny, hardly more than a mouthful each, and his hand was straying out again when his mother came back.

'Are you ever going to grow up?' she demanded.

Tim stared at her.

'I spent the entire afternoon making those for my committee's buffet party tomorrow night. Honestly, Tim, after tea at Aunt Dora's you shouldn't want anything to eat at all.'

Tim sighed.

'And now what's that puppy doing? She's got the end of the roller towel and there won't be any towel left in a moment. Do something with her.' His mother's eyes were furious, her colour high, both danger signals. Once, long ago, when one of his sisters had annoyed her, he'd made a storm cone, which was put unobtrusively on the landing window sill. His mother never did know what the brightly coloured triangular cone was for, but the rest of the family, seeing it, knew they had to be careful. Storm cone flying. It was still tucked away at the back of the big cupboard in Tim's room.

His mother walked out of the room and slammed the door.

Tim took the towel end, and pulled. The puppy, sure this was great fun, immediately pulled back. There was a rending noise, and Tim was left with most of the towel in his hands, the roller on which it had been held was on the floor, and the pup had dropped the ragged piece of towelling and picked up the wooden roller as being much more fun.

Tim tried to catch her but the more he ran after her the further she ran out of reach, enjoying the game immensely. Nobody had played with her like this at Aunt Dora's.

Desperate, Tim sat down on the floor and called to her.

She flew to him and climbed onto his knees, eager to be with him, enjoying seeing him so much reduced in size that he no longer towered over her, and cuddled on to his lap. She was tired after so much effort and fell sound asleep.

Tim leaned back against the kitchen counter, and picked up Aunt Dora's diet sheet; he didn't see how either he or the pup could return to the sitting room.

His father opened the kitchen door.

'Aunt Dora's done it this time, hasn't she?' he said. 'Did that long and difficult course of yours include looking after a dog?'

Tim looked at him.

'It included everything you can think of about a dog except how to feed it, groom it, train it, and live with it,' Tim said. 'I've only had her an hour and my mind's spinning. How come mother hates dogs and Aunt Dora's almost a dog herself?'

'Your mother's father bred dogs, your grandmother loathed them,' his father said. He opened the refrigerator door. 'Sausage rolls! Why on earth didn't your mother bring them in at tea time?' He took two and shut the door again.

Tim laughed. 'They're for her committee's buffet tomorrow; I've just got told off. Between the puppy and pinching mum's sausage rolls, life isn't going to be worth living until I go. Now you'll catch it.'

His father grinned too and opened the refrigerator door again. He took out two more rolls.

'Might as well be hung for a sheep as a lamb,' he said. 'Your mother's just like her grandfather, the Sea Captain. He thought he was running a ship in the Royal Navy till the day he died. He was always saying "I'll keep a tidy ship in this house; everything ship-shape and Bristol fashion; stand up, don't slouch, young man, get your hair cut, your room's a disgrace." I think your mother inherited his need for everything always to be under control. The last thing that's ever under control is a dog, until it's grown. We always had spaniels when I was young. Your grandfather used to shoot, and train his own dogs. Wish I'd listened to him a bit more, but I don't remember much about it. You'll have to go up to Aunt Dora and doss down on her settee for the next few days and soak up knowledge.'

It was an idea but not one that he cared for. The settee was old, the springs were broken and the dogs slept on it; several of them at a time, as well as Poohsey when he hadn't been 'abolished' to the big barn.

'Puppies need to go out when they wake up and after they're fed,' his father said, delving deep into long ago knowledge and coming up with one grain of useful information.

'How long do they sleep?' Tim wondered. It was a silly question. Why hadn't he been taught about feeding and training puppies? People coming to vets would surely ask about diet. He remembered a lecture on it vaguely, long ago, but he had no idea where the notes were. His father went out of the room and Tim continued to sit on the floor, long legs stretched, not wanting to wake the puppy, as he'd no idea what she would do when she did wake up. She seemed to have a remarkable capacity for mischief. His mother's immaculate home wasn't geared to puppies. He'd have been better off with her at Hell-hole Farm, which was what George had christened the pig farm. It didn't matter what happened in his bedroom there.

Zia was warm and furry and rather charming, even if she was a poodle. Her ears were silky to touch; her small nose damp and her closed eyes were slits giving her a slightly oriental expression.

He looked at her pedigree, picking out names of dogs and bitches he had known in the past. Her father's name was unknown to him; a completely different breeding kennel, except for one shared name five generations back. Aunt Dora, determined to teach her nephew everything she could, had written out a ten generation pedigree.

It must've taken her ages, Tim thought guiltily. There was nothing that Aunt Dora had forgotten to start him off properly. The diet sheet was comprehensive and took the pup up to eighteen months old. There was also advice on feeding during pregnancy. He had notes on that somewhere but he was sure they didn't agree with Aunt Dora's advice. She'd also added a list of herbal preparations useful in various illnesses. Oh Aunt Dora, Tim thought in despair. How do I tell my new boss that I don't want to use antibiotics; that she needs herbal tea; and that she has raspberry leaf tea to help her in whelping.

He hadn't even started his new career and he already had problems!

The puppy turned round in his lap and he held his breath. He needed a chance to think about her. There was nowhere for her to sleep; or was there? Aunt Dora had been outside for a remarkably long time. Had she put a dog bed in his boot? He would look when the pup woke up. A trip round the garden might solve one problem and teach her what she ought to do and where. And she'd have to learn all over again when he reached his new home.

There was an envelope pinned to the diet sheet and the pedigree form. He opened it and found her inoculation certificate inside; just the first injection. She would need a second and she couldn't mix with other dogs until she had had it, or she could still get distemper or hardpad or leptosirosis, that came from rats, and all of those illnesses killed. She couldn't go out to exercise yet where there were other dogs, which meant that if his new boss had a dog he'd have to find a place where other dogs didn't walk to exercise her.

Tim's father came back into the kitchen.

'Have you thought how you're going to manage for the next three days?' he asked.

Tim shook his head.

'Can you look in the boot of my car and see if Aunt Dora put anything in there? She seems to have provided everything the pup needs, but I don't know what to put her in to sleep.'

His father went out through the back door, careful not to make a noise. He'd seen the remains of the roller towel and the chewed roller. Tim tucked them out of sight; it wouldn't help as his mother was bound to notice the lack of a towel, of all things.

'Large container big enough for a young elephant,' Tim's father said, bringing in a huge polythene box without a lid, and dumping it on the kitchen floor. 'Once in that she won't get out. There's a woolly rug in it as well; and it's stepped, with a well and Dora's lined it with some sort of polythene sheeting and enough newspaper and kitchen rolls to mop up after a baby mammoth. There's a note; Aunt Dora's always a great one for notes.'

Tim took it. It was brief.

She's slept in this for a week and is used to it; she uses the paper at night; just burn it, and wash the polythene sheet. You can put her in it in the car

'She's thought of everything,' Tim said.

'There's this too,' his father added. He brought it into the kitchen. It proved to be a wire mesh sheet, with two hinges and two catches. It fitted neatly on top of the container making an enormous cage.

That would simplify life a lot. It would go on the seat at the back of the car; or he could take out the passenger seat and put it on the floor instead. He could put the pup in it tonight; and go to bed knowing she couldn't possibly get out.

'I wish I didn't know those sausage rolls were in the fridge,' Tim's father said, as he walked out of the room. Tim wished he hadn't been reminded. They were very tempting.

There was something else inside the container. A book on dog care: how to look after the dog daily, in illness as well as when it was well; and on training it and on its behaviour.

Zia woke, yawned, licked his hand and settled herself with a deep sigh against him. It was going to be impossible to resist her. She had no idea she wasn't his favourite breed. She already trusted him. She was a small bundle of warmth, something entirely his own and something alive. She would be company in the car when he went out on his visits; and if he had long drives to make she'd be fun to have with him.

He wondered if she would guard; she wasn't a guarding breed.

He looked at the book.

What is overfeeding for one puppy is starvation for another. No two are alike in what they need, even in the same litter.

That was a big help.

He looked at his aunt's diet sheet.

Give her exactly what I say for the first two weeks; then you will need to give more, but go easily or you will upset her; weigh her and base the increase on how much she gains.

He glanced down the sheet.

Breakfast: puppy milk which he had to make up according to his aunt's exact instructions. She had underlined **exact** in about twenty squiggles so that was obviously important.

Lunchtime was some kind of meat. She'd given him a bag of it but he might have to change to something different. *If so only change an ounce a day*, Aunt Dora wrote, ignoring metrication totally. *Take an ounce of the food I gave you and put in an ounce of the new food; mix it up so the taste is disguised. Then, if that agrees with her, two days later take out another ounce and put in two ounces of the different food. Don't hurry or she will have diarea.* His aunt had never been able to spell either. Anyway, who could spell diarrhoea. It was an idiotic word. And it was one thing he didn't want.

He had to give her more breakfast cereal at teatime and then milk before bed. She would have two raw eggs a week; she needed vitamin pills; and seaweed powder; and garlic pills; and she'd need worming until she was worm free. That was easy enough. He would find out for himself whether she had worms by looking down a microscope; there was sure to be one where he was going. He looked at the worm pills Aunt Dora had provided. He didn't approve of those for a start. He'd give her something much more modern when he got going on his own.

Zia needed four meals a day for another eight weeks. That was going to be a bit tricky; he would have to work out times that didn't interfere with surgery hours or operating. He hoped she wouldn't be car sick. She hadn't been on the trip from Aunt Dora's to his home.

Two meals a day by eight months; that would be easier to manage. She would probably have two for the rest of her life as she'd be out and about with him, and if she was exercised after a very big meal her tummy could twist and get a knot. Total cut off. They'd had a case of stomach twist in his last year. A bloodhound. The dog had died before they could operate. It was very nasty indeed.

People didn't always realise a dog must never be allowed to run on a very full stomach. They ought to teach anatomy of dogs and cats at school, Tim thought. So many people had them and so many people didn't even understand them. Come to that, nor did he. Nobody had lectured on training a dog to behave itself at vet college, or what went on in a dog's head.

He suddenly felt totally inadequate. He knew how to deliver a calf that was the wrong way round; he knew how to inject almost any creature under the sun. The last patient he'd had before leaving for Hellhole farm had been a turkey with pneumonia. The poor bird had looked dreadful, standing with its wings half raised and its head down, panting, its feathers shabby and miserable. That one had died but a second, brought in earlier for treatment had survived.

He'd always had someone to help him diagnose; now he was on his own. He had felt full of confidence until Aunt Dora gave him the puppy. That had removed every shred of confidence he'd had in about three hours. Puppies could get so many things wrong with them; teething problems; and inherited problems; and 'central heating' caused problems and 'too much cold' caused problems and there were infections that they picked up because they had no immunity to illness, the way children always get measles and mumps.

He wished he didn't know quite so much about that side of a dog.

Zia woke and rubbed herself against him. He put on her lead, with some difficulty because she thought it was meant to chew, and carried her outside. If he taught her to use the flowerbed instead of the lawn it might prevent problems later and he could cover everything she did. There was a big empty bed, dug over ready to receive roses when they came. His mother had had twenty rose trees as a present from his father on their twenty eighth wedding anniversary. His three sisters and their husbands had clubbed together to add another ten. They were ordered but hadn't arrived yet.

Zia liked the garden. She sniffed happily at the bushes, and was quite content to walk up and down the flower bed, occasionally jumping up at Tim to lick his hand. She found a dead leaf and picked it up, and carried it, intense concentration on her face. She dropped it to lie down and chew a stick.

'Supper, Tim,' his mother called.

'I'll be in in a minute.' Zia apparently had no intention of doing as his father said, and emptying herself after waking. The book had said she would, too. She obviously didn't read books or intend to do as books said she should.

At least she didn't mind the dark. Light spilled out of the big French window over the flower bed; the roses would be planted so that everyone could see them. Tim could see exactly what the puppy was doing.

She was digging a hole in his father's precious lawn, her small nose snuffling.

'No,' he said sharply and jerked the lead. Apparently that was what she needed. She sat and looked up at him engagingly, small head on one side, considering him. She pawed his leg appealingly.

'Oh, you,' said Tim in exasperation. 'Come on and be

good, do'.

'Tim!' His mother's voice was rising.

'I'm trying to get this puppy to empty itself,' he said.

'She obviously doesn't want to go. Bring her in,' his mother said. 'I want to get the meal over today, not tomorrow.'

'Giving Tim the puppy was a very good idea,' his father said, over her shoulder. 'A better idea even than Dora thought!' He knew very well that Tim had been full of his new degree, sure he knew everything now he had passed his exams; and that the puppy would soon convince him there was a lot more to it than just giving medicine. People would ask how to look after dogs; and how to train dogs; and how to stop them chewing the furniture and chewing the carpets and tearing up towels. He went into the kitchen and hunted for the roller and put it back in its place, then found a fresh towel from the kitchen drawer. He slipped out of the back door and tucked the torn towel into Tim's car. It would do for the dog; and with any luck his wife wouldn't see the teeth marks on the roller.

'Tim. Will you please put that wretched animal in her bed and come in and eat,' his mother yelled. 'Neither you or your father ever come for a meal on time.'

The welcome home had worn off, Tim thought, and went back into the kitchen. As he bent to pick the puppy up and put her in her bed she performed messily, on the floor.

'Oh, Lord,' his father said. 'Quick, I'll clean up. She must've finished. Where's the kitchen paper?'

Tim lifted the puppy and put her in her bed and fastened the lid over her. She didn't want to go to bed. She wanted to run riot and find another towel to tear. She wanted to explore and she wanted company, and began to whine. The whines changed to a whimper, and then to a squeal that reminded Tim of the piglets.

His father had mopped the floor. Tim tore off more paper, soaked it and washed the vinyl clean. By then his father had taken the tell tale evidence outside and buried it; they worked so fast that Tim was reminded irresistibly of the Keystone Cops and began to chuckle to himself. He found a spray and operated it, filling the kitchen with a most unlikely smell that he couldn't identify.

'I think you've just sprayed the room with your mother's new hair lacquer,' his father said. 'Come on, or we'll be in even hotter water. Do you think she'll ever shut up?'

They closed the door, after switching off the light.

Tim's mother was already eating. Their food waited for them, getting cold on the plates. One of her special hot meat loaves that Tim adored; and baked potatoes and peas and beans; and a lemon meringue pie.

They ate without speaking, all chance of conversation drowned by squeals from the kitchen. Whatever else she was, Zia was a most persistent pup.

'You can move that creature. I'm not washing up in that din,' his mother said, as they stacked the plates for her, anxious to make amends.

'Where can I put her?' There wasn't any likely place.

'Out in the car. In the river. Back with Aunt Dora. I neither know nor care so long as it's out of here,' his mother said. 'I never dreamed that a puppy could be so much nuisance.'

Tim went out the back door carrying the box. Zia, smelling him, tried to reach his hand and lick it, her small tail almost coming off in excitement and delight at being taken notice of again.

'What shall I do?' Tim asked his father in quiet desperation.

His father looked at him, and took his keys out of his pocket. A minute later the front door was opened and they checked the kitchen door. It was shut and the sound of clattering dishes being used as a protest against both of them sounded through the hall. Tim crept upstairs, carrying the crate.

'I've got to get her supper and take her outside again,' he said desperately to his father, as they stood together on the landing.

'I'll baby sit; no, better idea. I'll go out to the call box on the corner and ring Sue and ask her to invite us over for an hour or so. Your mother will be delighted to have a chance to see her new grandson again. And with the baby only eight weeks old, they aren't likely to be out.'

Tim went into his room. It hadn't altered since his schooldays. He grinned as he looked at his battered old teddy bear dressed in the Chelsea United colours, that Aunt Dora had given him when he was five. It was falling to pieces and had one ear only, and no eyes, but it was part of his life, and he was reluctant to throw it out. That was one thing that wouldn't be going with him.

The puppy was sitting watching him. He dared not take her out of the box in case she puddled; he wiggled a finger at her and she bit it, not in spite, but because it reminded her of milk and she was getting hungry again. He had a sudden thought and took her out, and put the box on its side, removing her bed, and laying the paper thickly. He replaced the lid; now the cage effect was even greater, but she could watch what he was doing and maybe that would keep her quiet.

He began to sort his books. He would take with him only those he wanted to re-read and the collection that his Uncle Sam had left him. Maybe his father would give him a decent book on dog training as a going away present.

He wouldn't learn anything about it from Aunt Dora as her dogs weren't trained, except to move properly in the ring and stand for the judge to inspect them. They ran riot and did as they pleased. He wasn't having Zia in septic tanks; she could learn to behave herself.

There was a tap on his door.

'Okay,' his father whispered and a moment later the phone downstairs rang. Tim grinned to himself and waited till the knock came again.

'Your mother asked me to tell you Sue's invited us over to see Mark have his last feed,' his father said. 'She wants to know if you'll be all right?'

Tim stifled an impulse to say that at twenty four he still needed a baby sitter, but grinned instead. His mother never would recognise that he'd grown up. Maybe mothers never did.

He waited till he heard the car drive away before returning to the kitchen. He took the box with him, and the pup watched him prepare her feed, becoming more and more excited, until she was trotting round the small enclosure in which she was penned, unable to wait for her milk. Tim was glad he hadn't taken her out as she puddled in excitement.

He took out the wet paper while she was feeding, making the most remarkable slurping noises as she drank. Her tail waved insistently; her long ears tended to dangle in the saucer. He would have to find a way of tying them up. He squatted down to watch her; and she turned and looked at Tim thoughtfully, identified him as the person who was going to look after her and feed her, and came to him and licked his hand. She trotted back to the bowl, to finish her feed. It looked lost in the big bowl Aunt Dora had given him, but by the time she was grown that bowl would be almost full.

He took her outside again and this time she did perform in the flower bed. He patted her head, and took her in. She was going to take up an awful lot of time at this rate and he had all his sorting and packing to do still. And he needed a new case; the mouse had done considerable damage to his old one and it smelled so musty that his mother had thrown it out.

He went upstairs and tucked the container down beside his bed. If she squealed maybe he could comfort her through the wire.

The puppy wanted to play. She'd been penned up for nearly two hours, and it wasn't much fun. He watched her romp round the room. She found a shoe and dragged it by the laces, then began to chew it. He removed that, and gave her a very holey old sock instead, which she carted about happily, dropping it to sniff at furniture, and then flopped on her side, suddenly and completely sound asleep. He picked her up, turned the container the right way up, and put her in her bed.

She could move in the night into the other half of the box if she woke. Presumably she understood about the newspaper.

Tim was exhausted. He went to bed, and when his parents came home there wasn't a sound from his room. Sleep came fast, and he dreamed of operating on a puppy that wouldn't lie still.

He woke in the dark to hear whimpers coming from the box.

'Oh, you,' he said in exasperation. He lifted her out, and cuddled her, sitting in his big arm chair with the pup tucked up on his knee. This was much better and she settled at once, warm and safe, held in strong arms, with a living breathing creature close to her, just as she'd had living breathing creatures close in the nest.

The book said never start it, but Tim was beyond caring. When he lived alone it wouldn't matter anyway what he did with his dog. He fell asleep, and only woke when sunlight flooded the room and the puppy was pushing hard at his nose, trying to wake him up.

'Oh, you,' he said again, and put her in her box while

he dressed and went downstairs to prepare her first feed and take her out. He discovered too late that he'd done everything the wrong way round. She should've gone out first.

In two more days they'd be off together, to a new world. He wondered just what that world would be like. He'd met his new employer at a London hotel; and had no idea exactly what sort of home he had, or what kind of practice it really was. 'Some small animals and some large animals; some horses; and some pigs and some chickens and some Ministry work; and some of all sorts,' the old man had said.

Though maybe he wasn't much older than his father. His father insisted fifty wasn't old. Tim tried to remember just what Mr. Fitzpatrick had looked like; a small burly man with a round red face and vivid blue eyes; with curly gray hair that clung round a bald patch exactly like a monk's tonsure; wearing thick tweeds, even though it had been a hot day, with a rather daunting habit of never answering at once when he was spoken to, but of considering every word, as if he were a judge about to pass sentence.

There had been one good thing about his new home.

'You'll have your own place and do your own cooking. You can keep whatever you like so long as it doesn't bother me. My last assistant had a habit of rescuing oiled seabirds and owls; not that the owls were oiled. They just seem to fall out of nests, or so he said. One before that kept goldfish. You and I will get on so long as you remember my wife doesn't like the practice interfering with her life; and so long as you do your share. And I pay on the nail and don't expect you to run up any debts in the area. It's cash business, all the time. Don't pay and they don't get their dogs from me till they do. You'll learn.'

Zia whined. She'd had enough of her box. Tim put on

her lead and took her outside into the sunlight, and watched her trot busily from place to place, investigating every inch with her small nose.

I wonder if I could teach her to track, he thought suddenly. I haven't got an Alsatian, but why shouldn't a standard poodle train just as well?

It was an intriguing thought; she was tracking from place to place and there was nothing wrong with her nose.

She came to him as he bent down to watch her, and climbed again into his arms, needing a tremendous amount of affection, partly because she was only a baby but mostly, though Tim did not realise it, because she was a dog that would need extra affection all her life, being far more attached to her owner than most animals, and determined to make sure she showed it.

Watching her, Tim wondered what their future would be together.

He would have been astounded could he see into the future, because she was going to lead him into a whole new way of life that he hadn't even thought of exploring when he started out to be a vet.

Chapter 4.

Zia, within the next two days, managed to chew the corner off a rug, damage the leg of a chair, steal a hot potato that dropped on the floor and burnt her mouth, and to generally turn the house upside down, so that Tim's mother saw him off with the greatest of pleasure and a fervent hope that by the time he came home for a weekend he would have the pup house trained and less liable to chew up everything in sight.

Tim's tiny car was loaded. He had removed the passenger seat and put the pup's large crate in its space. He'd made sure she was used to the car; it was far easier to drive around with her than to stay at home where she was constantly in trouble. He never seemed to stop saying 'No'.

No, she couldn't dig the lawn. No, she couldn't eat the dead leaves. No, that stick wasn't for chewing. He'd always looked at other peoples' dogs and thought that if he had a dog he would train it properly. How did you get the dog to understand? Zia had a built-in dislike of being shown what to do right; it was much more fun to do wrong.

He set off early as he had a long drive ahead.

It was a brisk day with a blowing wind, that made Zia excited. She didn't want to lie still in the car; she wanted to roam round her box and she wanted to climb on Tim's knee. She whined every time the car braked at traffic lights, and tried to climb out. He fastened the wire lid over the crate. She had to stay quiet while he drove, or she'd be dangerous.

Tim stopped to drink coffee from his flask, and let Zia wander round the car. She cuddled up against him and licked his hand. His ideas about poodles were changing fast. This was no pretty lady's pet; it was a strong-minded little animal with exactly the same instincts as any other dog. Treated in the same way it might well develop into something very good indeed.

Tim had looked up poodles in his book of dogs the day before. He was surprised to learn that they were first bred as hunting dogs and used to hunt in packs. The clipped coat was to prevent the curly fur being caught on brambles and the topknot had its own purpose. As white dogs were used, that soon became as dirty as the ground, the huntsmen tied a red ribbon on the topknot so that the dog could be easily seen if caught in brambles, which was the main hazard with their type of coat.

Poodles were always used in circuses because they were so easily trained. Zia was going to be trained. Tim had bought a book on training dogs, but since Zia couldn't read, and didn't know what the author said, she didn't seem to understand the methods used.

He stopped again in a lay-by and opened the lid of the crate. Zia jumped out and stood on Tim's lap, and nibbled his ear, biting painfully.

Tim shook her.

'Don't you dare do that to me,' he said to her crossly.

The pup looked at him, and leaned against him, her expression sorrowful. That she had understood. Her mother shook her when she was angry and her new master had done the same thing to her. She licked his hand, and when he put her back in her box, curled up meekly, and looked at him sideways.

Tim had found out by accident the best way to scold her. He realised that in future, if she did wrong, a little shake would do far more good then telling her NO. Maybe if he shook her and said NO at the same time, he could use the world alone in future. Up to now, she hadn't really realised what it meant.

As he let in the clutch to drive off, it dawned on him

that she was, after all, only sixty days old; it wasn't a very long a time in which to learn about the world. The trouble was that when a dog could race around like an adult animal you forgot it was only a baby.

The pup slept for the next seventy kilometres. Tim passed through big towns and small villages, and turned onto the motorway. The kilometres clocked up fast. He was beginning to feel nervous, wondering if he could manage his job. It was a bit like driving a car along for the first time. He would have to work out what was wrong with a dog, or a cat, or even a budgerigar. He would also have to learn to handle animals gently; his hands were large and sometimes he found it difficult, with a struggling animal, to be very careful with an injection. Dogs that had been hurt by the needle either turned very nervous next time, or might try to bite.

'Talk to the dog, man,' his Professor said, keeping up a stream of patter, like a conjuror showing tricks. 'There's a fine fellow then, this won't hurt, let's be having you up here; come on, don't be a baby, there's a good lad . . .' The dogs always seemed to relax with the Professor, whereas with Tim they tended to play up. Farm animals in some ways were easier, as you were rarely expected to cope with them alone. People expected you to be able to do anything with a dog or a cat, and he had vivid memories of trying to inject a Siamese cat that had all its claws and teeth embedded firmly in his arm. That had been remarkably painful and he'd had a sore arm for a very long time afterwards. Fortunately he'd already had his anti-tetanus injections, as did all who worked with animals.

By the time he reached the outskirts of the little town near which he was to work, he'd managed to worry about almost everything it was possible to worry about. It was all very well to have a degree in veterinary medicine and be able to write Member of the Royal

College of Veterinary Surgeons after your name, but it didn't seem to give enough confidence. He had horrible memories of George coping effortlessly with the cattle where he'd had to struggle; and of his farm boss meanly watching him battle to get the old horse out of the stable and then leading it out without any fuss or bother. Suppose every horse behaved like that for him? He'd be out of a job in no time flat.

He was suddenly very glad he had Zia for company. He stopped at the end of the lane to the surgery, and walked her in a newly ploughed field. He lifted her and held her against him, wondering if he would ever learn not to be so nervous about new places. He wished he had friends here; someone to talk to, to visit that night; someone to go out with; but he did have his dog. She was something of his own, and if he had no one else to talk to, he could talk to her.

He put her in her crate and fastened the lid securely. She would have to learn to stay there quietly while he was busy. He would have to learn to make a way of life that was easy for both of them. It might have been simpler without a dog, and such a young dog, but he would have a companion. He'd be able to walk her when he was free; to take her out in the evenings; to exercise with her.

The house was isolated, a large house standing by itself at the end of a long lane. The wrought iron gates which had once been very handsome, were now weathered and aged, but the rhododendron lined drive was immaculate, and beyond it were neat lawns and flower beds filled with chrysanthemums. It was not the sort of place in which he would dare to exercise the dog. A sign, beautifully painted and lettered, pointed to the back of the house. *Surgery*, with an arrow.

Tim drove round to the back. Here were white painted stables, but no horses. An open door showed a store room. A second door was obviously that of a small hospital; two cats were in large cages inside, lying on newspaper, obviously coming round from anaesthetics. A dog, tied to a ring in the wall, lay on a rug, and whimpered mournfully. A slim girl with dark hair came out of the room and shut the door.

'Surgery's over,' she said. 'There's another one at five tonight.'

'I'm Tim Yorke,' Tim said, and she grinned at him.

'The new assistant. Mr. Fitzpatrick had to go out to a calving. He told me to get you coffee when you came and show you where you were sleeping. Is that puppy a poodle?'

'A standard poodle. My aunt breeds them,' Tim said. He instinctively liked this girl; she was leading the way towards the far end of the stable block.

'This is our room; we don't go into the house. Mrs. Fitzpatrick isn't keen on animals so everything is kept quite separate. The surgery is just beyond the office; the waiting room beyond that. Most people come in the back way, past your cottage. That's it, over there.'

She pointed to a tiny two storied white cottage with small windows, like a child's drawing, at the furthest end of the stable block.

'This was once a little manor farm, with about six tied cottages. The house is really the old Hall; its gorgeous, but we don't ever go in. I live in one of the cottages with my husband; he works in one of the local banks, but we like it here. It's quieter than the town and the cottage is cheaper too. The other cottages are summer lets. The sea's only ten minutes drive from here. You'll be able to take your puppy on the beach in the evenings for a run; there are lovely long stretches of sand, when the tide's out.'

'I'm afraid I don't know your name,' Tim said, feeling at a disadvantage. She laughed.

'I'm sorry, I always forget. I'm Lisa Matthews. The other nurse is Tamsin Lincoln; and our receptionist is Sheila Grant. I expect you're tired after driving.' She poured boiling water onto instant coffee.

'Milk and sugar?'

'Please,' Tim said. He looked around him, at white painted walls, at the big desk, with an in-tray and out-tray, just like an office in a factory; at the filing cabinets against the wall; at the folders neatly stacked on the shelf, at the books on the far side of the room.

He went over to look at them as the telephone rang. *Know Your Horse. Sheep Husbandry and Diseases;* and other familiar titles from his college days.

He was aware of the telephone conversation behind him.

'Is the dog vomiting? No, don't give him anything to eat at all. Bring him over at once if you want to, as our assistant has arrived and he'll be able to tell you what to do. In twenty minutes? That's fine.'

Tim hoped he wasn't showing the dismay he felt; he wasn't prepared for his first case. His first case ever, on his own. Suppose he diagnosed something simple and the dog had distemper? Suppose it had something worse and he missed it? Suppose it was savage and it bit him?

He was being absurd and he knew it, but the nerves that had bothered him during the drive came back to plague him. He wanted so badly to do well at his job and he was afraid that he'd make awful mistakes all the time. Suppose the dog died because he'd diagnosed the wrong thing.

'What kind of dog is it?' he asked.

'It's only a pup; about six months old. It was very sick and she thinks it might be poisoned, but knowing her it's most unlikely. She does tend to fuss. We always ask them to come over though, if they're very worried. People get upset over their animals and if we can help we try; but without an assistant it hasn't been easy. The last one left five months ago to get married, and we haven't had anyone else since.'

Tim drank his coffee, and looked out at his cottage, wondering what it was like inside. He wanted to go and change; to take Zia out and give her a run and it was almost time for her food. He hoped the dog coming in was not infectious; he might infect his own pup afterwards.

He heard a car draw up, and a minute later the door bell rang. Lisa led him through a door at the back of the office into the surgery and handed him an immaculate white coat. It was slightly small but it hid his travelling clothes which weren't looking their best.

A fair haired woman with a desperately anxious expression on her face came into the surgery almost at a run, towed by a boisterous young labrador over which she had no control at all.

'He was terribly sick,' she said. 'It looked most peculiar, like dead leaves mixed up with blue of some kind; I'm sure he's been poisoned.'

Tim had never seen anything less like a poisoned dog. The labrador was busy sniffing every bit of the ground, while his owner pulled ineffectually at him, telling him to behave.

'He's a very naughty dog; he never does as I tell him. It isn't that he doesn't understand, because he does understand.'

Lisa had taken over while Tim studied his record card. The dog's name was Savager, which seemed an unwise choice; he wondered why they had chosen it. He'd been in for his inoculations: had come in once with a rubber band sunk deep into his leg, cutting it badly; had fallen out of the car; either he or his owner seemed rather accident prone. He'd had two attacks of vomiting, the first due to eating a whole kilo of liver which had been bought for their family meal, and the second due to one of the children letting him into the pantry where he had eaten everything in sight.

It must be a big family thought Tim who hated liver.

He knelt beside the dog, and promptly found his face being licked all over.

'Behave yourself,' he said firmly only to see Lisa, behind the owner's back, with a warning finger on her mouth. Touchy owner he decided. He asked Lisa to hold the dog still and carefully felt his tummy. No sign of any trouble there.

Taking his temperature was far from easy. All of them had to hang on to him as he determinedly tried to investigate this thing that was sticking under his tail.

No temperature.

'The dead leaves probably caused the trouble,' Tim said. 'He seems to be perfectly all right now; no sign of trouble, but I'll give him something to soothe his tummy. Have you anything blue in the house that he could've eaten? My puppy ate half a towel the other day.'

'Have you a puppy?' the woman asked. Tim had obviously risen considerably in her estimation. If he had a dog too, he must know about dogs. She was prepared to consider the possibility that her dog had eaten something undesirable if the vet's did the same thing. Tim watched as she relaxed, visibly.

'My blue hankie,' she said. 'It was that colour. I hadn't thought of that. You're sure there's nothing really wrong? Not poison? Nor a germ? There are some very nasty germs about and my sister's puppy. . . .'

'I promise you,' Tim said, quite sure that this animal, so obviously full of life and health, couldn't possibly have anything more than an upset due to eating things not meant for dogs to eat. He handed her the bottle of kaolin mixture Lisa had taken off the shelf.

'Put the right dose of that in his feed tonight; and come back if you have any more problems. I'm sure there's nothing to worry about this time. Young dogs eat all kinds of things.' He thought of Zia's efforts in the last two days. She'd given him more experience in dogs in that time, than he'd had in five years of training. Living with a dog was very different from seeing it in the surgery for a few minutes.

Lisa led the client out, and watched her being rushed to the car, the dog anxious to get away from the man who stuck unpleasant things under his tail. Tim washed the thermometer, and put it in sterilising fluid.

'Your pup is going to be a major benefit,' Lisa said. 'Mr. Fitzpatrick has no animals as his wife doesn't like them, and people think that means he doesn't know anything about them. At least,' she added, 'he hasn't animals here. He has a spaniel that he keeps at his brother's place and trains for field trials. And he grew up with dogs. But if you have a puppy and can re-assure some of our puppy owners about its behaviour, it'll help a lot. Did you see how she changed, from being a bit awkward to being interested in your pup?'

Tim nodded. He hadn't thought of Zia as being of use in that way before, but obviously people would listen to him far more if they thought he knew what they were talking about from his own experience.

'I've only had her a few days,' he said.

'We've three dogs at home, Yorkshire terriers; Toby, Pip and Squeak. We don't keep them in their show coats; they're clipped and look much sweeter that way, I think. They're remarkably naughty and that helps too. If you have a dog there's always something to talk about, even with the shyest owner, and they do relax if you start to talk about your dogs.'

Tim hoped there'd be no need to see anyone else. He was stiff from sitting too long and he wanted to feed Zia.

He wanted to see his new home. He was hungry and would have to get some kind of meal. Luckily he'd lived in a flat with three friends during his last two years in college and knew how to cook and cater. They'd taken it in turns; one shopped one week, while the second cooked, the third washed up and the fourth had a week off. It had worked extremely well except for Bill's cooking week, as his idea of food was nothing but baked beans on toast and bacon sandwiches; the rest of them had been more ambitious.

'Come and see your new home,' Lisa said, guessing his thoughts. 'The phone has an amplifier outside so that we can hear it wherever we are. You have an extension and there's an extension in almost every room. It saves time and we get emergencies quite often. It's a very busy place.'

She led the way across a cobbled yard, through a wicket gate, and into a small untidy garden.

Tim was relieved to see that his garden was fenced all the way round with chestnut fencing, as he'd discovered Zia had the ability to wriggle through the smaller gaps.

There was no way she could escape from this. There was a rough lawn in need of cutting, and edgings of flower beds.

The front door led straight into a tiny sitting room, furnished with two big armchairs, a table and three dining chairs, a large rug on a wood block floor, which was obviously much newer than the cottage, and bright chintzy curtains and covers. One wall was shelved and would be perfect for his books. There was a picture of a sailing clipper on the second wall, and of a galloping horse on the third. He had his own pictures to add to that.

The kitchen, though equally tiny, was modern, and a great improvement on the one in his college flat where the ancient cooker had taken three times as long as it should've to cook anything. To his surprise there was a microwave oven on the counter at the far side.

'It makes it easy to heat things up if you've been out all night,' Lisa said. 'We all have them; it saves hours of cooking. Mr. Fitzpatrick has everything geared to maximum efficiency; which means we have to be jolly efficient, or we're in really hot water. No oversleeping; no failing to answer the phone, or not being here when needed; and night calls have to be answered immediately or else. I hope you don't sleep too soundly.'

Tim was aware that he was tired and being told too much all at once. He wasn't taking it in. Lisa, realising this, turned to go.

'I cooked you a cold meal and made a salad; it's hard on the first night to have to set to and make food,' she said, and went out. Tim opened the cupboard and stared at a huge pasty, a dish of beetroot, another of coleslaw, and a bowl of green salad, as well as a cold apple pie, a jug of cream, a new baked brown loaf, with a packet of butter beside it, a jar of instant coffee, a bottle of milk, and a large fruit cake. He cut a slice of that and wolfed it down; he'd eat properly later.

He felt a great deal more cheerful as he went upstairs, to find that his bedroom stretched the whole length of the cottage; was furnished with a bed, an armchair, a wall of cupboards to hold his clothes; and was a total contrast to the room he'd slept in on the farm.

That seemed centuries ago.

He also had a well equipped modern little bathroom, with a shower instead of a bath, no doubt to add to his efficiency he thought with a grin. There was never much temptation to laze in the shower, whereas it was always tempting to soak in a hot bath after a bad day.

He whistled as he walked down the stairs again and out to his car to bring Zia in to explore her new home.

He still had to meet his boss and find out more about

the place but his nerves had almost vanished, and were replaced by excitement.

Chapter 5.

Zia was bored. She was hungry and Tim had left her too long alone. She tried to wriggle free from the wire lid over her crate, but failed, so she decided to call him instead. Long wails pierced the air, and Tim raced out to his car. He had left it in the drive behind the house.

The woman standing beside the car was dark haired, tall, and very elegant, in cream trousers, with a cream silk blouse, and a dark cardigan. The glowing jewel on the pendant round her neck was a vivid scarlet against the cream. Her dark eyes were angry.

'Do you have to leave that dog there, making such a noise? Surgery times are very clearly written on the plate by the gate.'

'I'm sorry,' Tim said.

'Then go,' and she turned away from him and walked towards the house, leaving Tim totally at a loss for words.

'That's Mrs. Fitzpatrick,' Lisa said, coming up behind him. 'She doesn't like animals. Which sometimes makes life difficult. Can you shut the puppy up?'

'She's fed up,' Tim said, opening the car door and lifting the puppy out of her crate.

'What a beauty,' Lisa said in delight. 'We don't have any standard poodles on our list. My father used to breed them. He used them instead of spaniels as gundogs, as they do in America. Everyone thought he was crazy but they had to admit he got results. Two of his won field trials.'

She squatted down and flicked her fingers, and the pup ran to her, tail wagging exuberantly.

'My aunt gave her to me,' Tim said. 'I couldn't say no. It would have caused a rift for ever in the family.' He looked down at Zia, who was thoughtfully scratching her ear, a blissful expression on her face. Her legs seemed to have lengthened visibly in the few days that he'd owned her.

'No problem,' Lisa said. 'If I'm not on duty, I'm your next door neighbour, so she can either be with us in the office, or with me in the cottage, or with you in the car, or else, when she's older, you can use the big kennel. We all put our dogs there from time to time, when we're busy, or there's an emergency, or we go on holiday and can't take the dogs. It's over here,' she added and led the way to a big barn. The inside had been converted into a row of kennels, each with its own run, its own bed placed on a shelf of wood at the back, and with heating overhead for winter.

'We used to board dogs here, but we had to stop as they do get noisy at times,' Lisa said. 'Ours have to be very well trained or we get complaints from Madam.'

'Why ever did she marry a vet?' Tim asked.

'They met in wartime; he was in the Air Force. She didn't realise what his job involved till he started in practice. I think she always hoped he'd become a desk man and work for the Ministry with proper hours of work, but he's terrific with animals; it would be a crime for him to be desk-bound. He's passionate about them. Don't you ever skimp on any beast; that's the only thing that really does make him mad. That and R.S.P.C.A. cases. He'll love Zia, so don't worry. We manage very well, so long as we remember the rules, but whatever you do, don't ever let her run into their garden. That's sacred; it's open to the public once a year, so we all go out then, to leave it free of any hint of animals. It's a Sunday so no problem. No dog may lift a leg anywhere or bitch squat on the lawn; it has to be perfect and so does the house. You'll probably find that Mr. Fitzpatrick comes over to you quite often to relax. He'll call it talking business. He's a nice man to work for.' Lisa was working while she spoke, counting the various preparations on the shelves, and marking down the numbers in a notebook.

'This is one of my jobs for today. We try to keep everything as well organised as we can, but of course it's not that kind of job. . . . Trypsin substitutes; we've several dogs who are on one or the other because of pancreas trouble. There's a lovely golden retriever, he's a darling, he's been having treatment for nine years. He can't digest meat – none of them can. We've got several different preparations here; we have to see which suits which dog.'

'I thought they didn't live all that long,' Tim said, his only experience brief and mostly from books.

'So the books say, but animals, luckily, don't read, and Goldie never realises he isn't as fit as the next dog. He lives a perfectly normal life, except for having his enzyme substitute added to his food every day. After all, diabetics live for ever on insulin and lead normal lives. . .

Vitamins; we need more of those – and we're out of puppy milk. Mr. Fitzpatrick keeps the pups on it till six months old. The kind we have here is excellent; makes lovely bone, if the breeder has done the rearing job properly. We have the usual problems here, with people selling for money and not caring what they sell. I wish people would look for dogs before they buy. Trouble is puppies sell themselves. Damn, there's the phone.'

She put down the notebook with a sigh. Tim looked at the shelf; she had just started counting a vast number of little phials of eye and ear drops and would have to begin again when the call was finished.

'A cat for neutering? Yes, we can do that. Just let me check the book. How old is he?'

Lisa flicked her fingers and Tim looked around, and

saw a large hardcovered book lying on the far desk. He brought it over and she opened it, scanning down the pages.

'Thursday morning at ten? Can you bring him in at nine thirty, please. No food from five o'clock onwards the day before and no water after 9 p.m. You can ring us at three to find out when to collect him. What's his name?'

Zia was trotting busily round the room inspecting everything. The floor was of wood block, which appeared to interest her immensely. She tried to pick up one of the blocks in her mouth, and then sat and looked at it, her head on one side, as if baffled by the impossibility. She trotted over to Tim and sat and looked up at him.

'That one's Siamese. He'll probably be your job; so we're in for a noisy day next Thursday,' Lisa said. 'They always make a terrific din, which usually sets off the other animals. That sounds like Mr. Fitzpatrick's car; so I suggest you take some paper towelling and mop that up quick before he sees it. Zia's leaked in the corner. You'll have to do better than that.'

She threw a paper towel across the room and Tim mopped hastily. He should have been watching; he should've taken her out into his cottage garden; he should have done all kinds of things with her but he was so fascinated in finding out all he could about his new job that he'd completely forgotten.

The car was a beaten-up Land Rover with a soft top, much to Tim's surprise. He'd seen the expensive foreign car in front of the house and assumed that his employer would drive something similar. His boss, at home, seemed a different man to the sombre-faced person he had met in the hotel.

'So you've arrived. There's another Land Rover for you to drive round the farms,' Mr. Fitzpatrick said, erupting into the room rather like a small explosion. 'Lisa, have you done those orders yet? Any phone calls, any emergencies, what's this then? Vomiting dog. Who saw it, did you see it, Tim?'

'Tim saw it, Fitz,' Lisa said.

'The girls always call me that,' he said, turning to Tim. 'We had a student here a few years back, to see practice, who didn't know what to call me. Mr. Fitzpatrick is a mouthful, so he called me Fitz, and the name seems to have stuck.'

He laughed and turned to find Zia sitting in front of him, looking up at him with pleading eyes.

'Yours, or have we acquired it?' he asked. He backed away without waiting for an answer.

'Come on then, puppppppp,' he called, and Zia, delighted to be noticed, ran over to him as he squatted on his heels to make himself less alarming to her.

'My aunt gave her to me,' Tim said. 'I didn't know how to say no. I couldn't; she meant well.'

'Damn sensible woman,' Fitz said. He rubbed the pup's ears and she rolled over, paws in the air, asking for her tummy to be rubbed. 'Nothing like a man who has a dog of his own to give the pet owners confidence and you won't give damn silly advice about house-training, because you'll have learned it isn't all that easy the first time round. And you can join the dog club.'

'I can do what?' Tim asked, too amazed to remember to be polite. He'd never in his life heard such a horrible idea. He had visions of himself as the only man, and a man with a poodle at that, with dozens of elderly ladies all drinking tea and talking about their dogs as if they were babies.

'It's a very good club,' Fitz said, taking a packet of peppermints out of his pocket and handing them round. 'I don't smoke; tomfool habit, and anyway animals don't like the smell of tobacco and if your nose is full of cigarette smoke, you miss on a smell that might be important in diagnosis. You need clean hands and a good nose and good head on this job. And no funny ideas about not working at night or in the evening. The job comes first. No use leaving a cow to die while you finish your supper. I've had two assistants leave me because they couldn't take the hours. Girl friends want attention and that's it. I don't want you falling in love; no time for love in our job.'

He glanced again at the book.

'What was wrong with that dog? Eaten her tights?'

'No,' Tim said. 'Dead leaves and a handkerchief.'

'At least it got rid of them,' Fitz said. He took off his tweed jacket and put on one of the white coats, then took it off again. 'There's a dirty mark on the front of this; we'll start surgery clean.'

Lisa winked at Tim and took down a second coat. Tim couldn't see any mark at all on the first.

'You can work beside me, and get to know a bit about my methods,' Fitz said. 'And no nonsense when you tell the clients what to do. Make it brief, make it simple, and if they waste your time, charge double. Otherwise you find you spend the whole night with a dog with toenails that need clipping, and Lisa can do that anyway in her own time.'

Tim followed him into the surgery, feeling more than a little bemused.

Lisa herself, now wearing a white coat, went out into the waiting room.

Tim looked around the surgery; a big bare room with an examination table, two counters under which were drawers and shelves and a trolley holding the instruments, thermometers, and a steriliser.

On one wall was a large chart with different breeds of cattle; on the next were sheep and horses; and the third wall held charts of cats and dogs. A large notice said NO

SMOKING and another said CASH ONLY. NO CREDIT. A girl Tim hadn't seen before came into the room; she was tiny but as she turned, Tim realised she was older than her height admitted.

'I'm Tamsin,' she said, as she went over to the desk and took out a card. 'First patient is Mr. Griffiths, but it's not his dog. It's his duck; we haven't seen it before.' She laid a fresh card down on the table.

The man who came in was small, bearded and unexpectedly young. For some reason Tim had expected an old man.

'Fox got it,' the bearded man said, untucking the duck from the towel he'd wrapped it in. It clattered its beak, flapped its wings and hissed.

'How did you get it away?' Fitz asked, his hands busy with the bird. It relaxed, as he spoke, and looked up at him, miserably huddled into its feathers.

'I have a stallion in the field; Midnight; you know him. He galloped over and kicked the fox in the ribs; never seen anything like it. That's a fox that won't go duckhunting for a long time and probably never in my field. What's the damage?'

'A broken leg.'

Tamsin was already beside him with splints and bandages. Tim watched Tamsin's expert hands fasten the splints, by which time the syringe was ready for an injection.

'Rest it in a box of straw; that leg should heal all right. Pay Lisa as you go out.'

The man and the bird vanished through a second door that Tim hadn't noticed and Fitz punched a bell on his desk, for his second client to come in.

Tim was tired and he hadn't had time to eat properly, just that slice of fruit cake. He thought longingly of food and bed: it had been a long day as he'd started out at dawn and had driven over four hundred kilometres.

He helped tie a bandage round the mouth of a snarling dog that had an overwhelming desire to bite everyone in sight; he held a cat, and was scratched for his pains. The cat had an infected rat bite on its hind leg and was in pain. He was a big black Tom with a torn ear, and as the needle went in he yelled at the top of his voice, an enraged scream of indignation and fright.

Two puppies came in last, when all the other clients had gone, for their protective inoculations. The first was a tiny Yorkie, with bright eyes and an engaging cheeky face. Fitz squeaked at him and he sat, head on one side, looking at this man who made such funny noises. Fitz tickled his ear, and scratched his chest and then cuddled him up against him, talking to him, and the needle was in and out so fast the baby hadn't even noticed.

'No fear there if you do that the first time,' Fitz said.

The second puppy was a St. Bernard, an enormous floppy little bitch that seemed to be all legs that refused to do what she wanted. She sat on the floor as if someone had spilled her there, rolling over on one side. Fitz knelt down to her and she flapped a paw at his face. He clucked and made squeaky noises and once more the needle was in and out without a murmur from the pup.

'Very important not to scare them stiff by being rough. Baby puppies remember bad experiences all their lives and one piece of rough handling will make sure dogs hate coming back.

You can't always avoid it; they remember being left for an operation and make a fuss next time in case you go away. But with luck those two won't need any treatment other than boosters every year to make sure they're always protected against distemper. We get too many cases here among people who don't realise puppies should be inoculated. Funny, they'll pay £150 for a dog and then complain at £7 or so for the injections to keep the dog alive. In the old days they died like flies, and if you get it in a kennel with pups in the nest you get real trouble; they lose all the puppies.'

Surgery was over at last, but the day's work wasn't yet done. The books had to be made up; the cards filled in; the money balanced and put in the safe; the surgery had to be cleaned and the waiting room too, ready for morning. There were two cats in the hospital to be fed and the paper in their cages renewed. One of them had been run over and the dressing needed changing on a very nasty wound on his leg. Tim bathed it and re-bandaged it; the cat was used to the procedure and remarkably co-operative.

'This is when we pray the phone won't ring, at least till Fitz has had his supper,' Lisa said, as she put away the cleaning tools. 'Today's not been too bad. Some days you end up wanting to scream and never see another animal as long as you live. Specially if it's been a farm day, and out to pigs or cattle in the fields, and it's sure to be pelting.'

'Where's Zia?' Tim asked, suddenly terrified in case she'd escaped and lost herself.

'I got nosy and went over to your cottage and found her diet sheet; you'd put it in a conspicuous place; I thought you would. She's been fed; she's been a good clean girl, and she's in her crate in your car, sound asleep. We do know about animals here, you know,' she added, and Tim laughed.

The phone rang on the desk.

Lisa answered.

'Okay. I'll tell him.' She hung up. 'Fitz will do all the night calls, so long as there aren't two emergencies at once; so go to bed and sleep. Make sure you're up early; shall I ring you? All our phones interconnect.'

'Good idea,' Tim said. All he could think about was food, a shower and bed. But he had to fetch Zia and she'd need to go out before he could finally call it a day.

He yawned massively.

Zia would have to learn to sleep in her crate downstairs; he hoped she wouldn't howl in the night. He went to his new home and switched on the light. Tomorrow, if he'd time, he'd put out his own things and make it much more his. Tonight, all he wanted was sleep.

He ate standing up, looking out into the darkness. If he sat down he would fall asleep. He was glad he'd never started smoking. It would be no hardship at all to obey that rule. He liked to keep himself very fit and that meant no smoking at all. He wondered if there was a boys' club somewhere; he might coach them in boxing; that would be fun.

The dog club!

Maybe he could make sure that that was the night for surgery so that he couldn't go! He didn't like the thought at all. He'd never been near a dog club; and had no idea what went on, but he felt it would be impossible to go and sit and drink tea or coffee and eat biscuits and talk about dogs. Maybe they had lectures. . . . he couldn't imagine what they did.

Zia was bumbling round her box, complaining. He hadn't spent nearly enough time with her today. He lifted her out and took her into the dark garden, where she discovered a molehill and decided to dig down and find its inhabitant. There was nothing there, and she trotted off into the darkness.

A moment later Tim heard her cry out as if she had been hurt. He whistled and she raced to him so fast she fell at his feet in a sprawl of legs. He bent down. Her face was covered in earth as if someone had thrown a handful at her; her eyes were almost blocked.

Furious, he took her in, and began to sponge her down.

Lisa knocked at the door.

'Can I come in?' she called.

'Fine,' Tim said. He didn't turn his head but went on sponging the pup's face. 'Look what someone's done to her! What sort of people do you have around here, for heaven's sake?'

Lisa laughed.

'It's not funny,' Tim said. 'Suppose there'd been stones there; she'd have been blinded.'

'Calm down,' Lisa said. 'It was a mole. We've dozens of them. My dogs are always getting into the same sort of mess, but they do learn. He must've come up under her nose and scattered earth into her face. I'll get some drops to soothe her eyes from the dispensary. Don't forget to pay, though.'

She was back in a few minutes with a little phial. Zia shook her head as the drops went in. She didn't like them at all. She blinked and her eyes flooded with tears.

'She's okay. I came in to ask if you've everything you need. Your half day off is tomorrow, so you'll be able to go into town and stock up. Make a list as we don't often get much chance to shop. There's a deep freeze, a little one, outside your back door in the utility room. That's another place where Zia would be safe and out of hearing of the house if she did kick up a row. The freezer flex is right behind it, out of her reach, and there's nothing else there she can possibly damage unless you take to leaving shoes and wellingtons in there. You'll have to teach her not to chew.'

Tim was glad when she'd gone. He'd never been so tired in his life, not even after exams; but he was working at last, and he liked Lisa and Tamsin; he liked his cottage, and Zia was going to be far less of a problem than he'd thought.

Also he liked Mr. Fitzpatrick; he was a different man here on his home ground and much nicer than Tim had expected. On the other hand, he hadn't taken to Mrs. Fitzpatrick at all. It was going to be necessary, all the time, to make sure he didn't upset her, and by the look of things she'd be upset by almost anything that interfered with her well-ordered life.

He took Zia outside again just before midnight. He had put on the television set briefly and fallen asleep, to wake up when the programme was over. His back ached; he was too tall for this chair and would have to buy another that fitted him better.

He went up to bed at last, leaving the puppy in her crate. She settled down at once, in spite of her strange surroundings, as she had her own den to sleep in so nothing was so different for her.

Tim switched on his bedroom light and turned back the bed – to discover a neat pile of blankets with two sheets and a pillow case on top.

Wearily, he set to to make it. He should have thought. It would be easier tomorrow; he would know his way round; he'd begin to work; he would house train Zia; he would. . .

His plans drifted into dreams.

He slept without moving, totally exhausted, and woke with a jump when the telephone rang. It couldn't be morning.

'Sorry Tim,' said Fitz's voice. 'There's a difficult calving. I've been here alone but I need help. Tamsin will be waiting for you with her car to bring you out here. See you.' He rang off and Tim stumbled around in the dark to find the light switch and dress.

The door bell sounded as he came downstairs. Zia was crashing round in her box greeting him excitedly and his heart sank. She'd need food and to go out. . .and he hadn't time.

Both Lisa and Tamsin stood in the doorway, Lisa in her dressing gown.

'We're a team here,' she said. 'I'll see to Zia. You get off.' He was in the car and Tamsin was away, foot hard down, driving full pelt down the lane, her headlights cutting through the darkness. She said nothing, and Tim dozed off, wishing he was back in his bed again.

He'd begun his new life with a vengeance.

Chapter 6.

Tamsin drove fast, expertly and in total silence. Tim, waking out of his doze, watched the headlights pick up trees and hedges. Once they drove gently through a flooded part of the road, where the ditch on one side seemed to have met a little pond on the other side with unpleasant consequences. A notice beyond it said TEST YOUR BRAKES and Tim shot forward in his seat as Tamsin obeyed.

'Nothing wrong with them,' she said with satisfaction, and changed gear to climb a winding hill that appeared to lead straight into the sky. Tim wasn't used to mountainous country. The headlights picked up a sheep and a cow wandering along the road, and then the white of a painted five barred gate, leading into another lane.

Tim opened the gate, waited for the car to pass through and shut it again. He could hear voices ahead.

Tamsin drew up in a cobbled yard.

'Your boss is up here,' a man's voice called, as he approached from behind a barn. There was a little light in the sky. It would soon be dawn. The glow from one of the practice's big handlamps shone surprisingly from somewhere up above the roof of the barn.

Tim walked round the barn and the farmer shone his own handlamp.

Tim stared in disbelief.

Fitz was perched, unhappily and not very safely, on the ledge of an outcrop rock that towered over the barn. A ladder led up to it, and beside him, held firmly back against the cliff face by his body and that of another man, was a 'very much in calf' cow, bellowing at the top of her voice.

'The calf's nearly here,' Fitz called down. 'The only

problem is that we can't reach round her and when it comes it's going to crash down the cliff and kill itself. Ivan can't come up as it needs someone to steady the ladder and there's no one else around to do it. He's going to move the ladder; he and Tamsin can hold it steady as it's not going to be exactly safely balanced for you, and somehow you've got to get that calf down to them; we've rigged up a sacking sling; there's just room behind her for you to stand. I hope you've got a good head for heights.'

Tim looked on in astonishment. He had delivered calves in the veterinary hospital and in barns and byres, but he'd never delivered a calf on a ledge perched precariously above a three metre drop onto hard ground. Calves wriggled; and if the cow slipped, down would come cradle and baby and all.

He shook himself awake.

'It strikes me I'd be better learning mountain rescue than veterinary medicine,' Tim said, as the farmer and Tamsin steadied the ladder. He climbed three rungs and slipped.

'Better with your shoes off,' Tamsin suggested, and Tim climbed down and removed both shoes and socks; he would be better barefoot but the chill of the ground made him clench his teeth. What on earth had he wanted a job like this for? In his next life he'd be a bank clerk. They didn't climb ladders in the dark. And the cow had managed a few cowpats while she was there, which didn't help matters at all.

She bellowed loudly and continuously, desperate with fear. There was no way she could be lowered until the calf was safely born. Tim wondered how she'd got there but was too busy dodging her swishing tail to ask. He might get a mouthful of muck and that was last thing he wanted.

He reached the ledge at last and was relieved to see

there was more room behind the cow than he'd thought. Fitz and the cowman had managed to turn her so that she backed onto a tiny platform, on which straw had been spread, so that Tim had a foothold.

He could see the calf already striving for birth.

'We've been praying she wouldn't let go till you came; it could roll so easily,' Fitz said. He was plastered in muck, and his shirt was torn. The grey light of dawn was growing on the horizon, which was far beyond them, above the crags. The hills were black jagged shapes, softened by cloud. It was going to rain.

The cow bellowed suddenly and loudly and the calf came free, sliding into Tim's arms. He moved slightly as the cow kicked out. Fitz slipped and swore. The cowman was muttering to himself and Tim didn't think his speech was complimentary.

He wished his feet weren't so cold as he knelt by the little animal and tore the membrane away from its head so that it could breathe.

Should he wait a few minutes or lower it at once? If it began to move it might slip out of the sling or hurt itself. It twitched an ear and sneezed. It was alive, and he put the sacking round it and fastened the ropes. There was an old tyre lying by the sacking, and that too he fastened to the calf's side, to keep it from banging against the cliff face.

'Ready,' he called. 'It's alive and looks well.'

'Ready,' the farmer said from below, and Tamsin angled the handlamp into the air. Tim moved, and discovered he was in a very awkward position indeed for lowering even a bag of potato crisps, let alone a very heavy and unmanageable newborn calf.

If he stood up and bent over he would overbalance. All he could do was lie flat and push gently. He lowered himself into the mucky straw, wishing he had a gas mask. It was unbelievably cold and unbelievably slimy.

He found it extremely difficult to push the calf forward slowly; he didn't want it to drop suddenly over the edge. Gently, gently, he whispered to himself, aware of the cow's hind hooves right in front of his face. If she moved backward she would stand on his face, which wouldn't improve his appearance at all.

Gently, gently, holding onto the ropes with all his strength. He was suddenly aware of Tamsin's face, level with his at the top of the ladder. She reached out both hands to steady the calf, and helped him ease it to the edge of the little shelf, and then, very gently, over the side, paying out the rope slowly. She disappeared and Tim eased himself to look down. She was balancing the weight of the calf, keeping the tyre against the cliff face, as Tim lowered. She was much stronger than she looked, he thought, as the weight of the animal tore at his shoulder muscles and the rope bit into his hands.

The weight was off him. The farmer had reached up and taken it on his own hands and arms, and then the calf was down on the ground. Tim stood, wondering if he would slip from the ladder, as he was covered in slime. He climbed down.

'Calf's fine. Tamsin's seeing to it,' the farmer said. 'Now what do we do about the old devil herself?'

'How did she get there?' Tim asked.

'Fell from above. The ground's flooded and muddy and she slipped and then couldn't stop. Lucky she ended up there and didn't crash into the yard or I'd have lost both of them. As it is, I can't see how we can get her down. It'll be difficult to get the slings on her and lower her from there; and we can't get a crane up our lane. Or a fire engine and ladder.'

He watched Fitz edge round the cow, and peer down at him. Tim looked around him. There was hay, stacks of hay, in the barn.

'Suppose we pile the ground thickly with hay and try

to lower her?' Tim said. 'If you put ropes round her she might try and clamber down and then end up in soft hay instead of on hard ground.'

'Worth a try,' Fitz called down, his body jammed against the cow who now knew she'd had a calf and wanted to get to it. Tim had a horrible vision of both man and cow crashing earthwards.

The tractor was brought out and the trailer attached. Tamsin, Tim and the farmer hauled bales of hay, working as fast as they could. Tim ached all over. It would soon be surgery time; people would have to wait.

Tim prayed there were no other emergencies waiting for them. The hay was taken out of the trailer and spread over the ground, carpeting it densely close to the little cliff. Seen by daylight it wasn't so high; but it was formidable with a cow stuck up on it, and she needed attention after calving. He went up the ladder with ropes and sling; it wasn't going to be easy.

The cow had no idea she was being helped. She decided she was about to be slaughtered and her head moved threateningly as she tried to push the cowman off the ledge. Fitz took the opportunity to slip the sling under her; he fastened it, with extreme difficulty, balancing on one leg, using one hand, his other hand clinging to the only bush in sight, which he prayed would not give away under his hands. Tim, watching, held his breath, wondering if human treatment was the same as veterinary when it came to broken bones. Humans were such an odd shape he thought suddenly and grinned.

'It's not funny,' Tamsin snapped at him.

'I know; but my lack of experience is,' Tim said ruefully, 'I was just thinking that humans are an odd shape and I know how to splint a cow's leg, but human legs are quite different.'

'All we need is a nut,' Tamsin said. 'We've had practically everything else in the way of assistants.'

Tim knew he'd never be able to explain. Some people took remarks quite the wrong way; they didn't seem to understand the simplest thing at times. He knew what he meant and it wasn't nutty, it was funny. Oh well.

He thought of his mother's expression, if she could see him now, covered from head to foot in muck and slime, barechested and barefooted in straw, waiting for a cow to be lowered to him. If he had dreamed it and told them his dream they'd have thought it unlikely; but it was far from unlikely. He had straw piercing his foot, and his toe was bleeding. He could hear the calf calling and the cow was now bawling in answer, and Fitz was making ferocious noises and the cowman appeared to have gone quite mad, as he was hauling on the cow's hindlegs.

A moment later, Tim saw why, as she slid gently off the ledge, held by the ropes; both men were leaning back against the cliff; and one of the ropes was firmly round a bush which was levering slowly out of its bed.

The cow, finding herself in the air, no solid ground under her, made so much noise that other cows started to answer her; a dog barked dementedly and the calf cried for its mother.

Merry heaven, Tim thought, but didn't say it. He went forward with Tamsin and the farmer, and reached towards the cow. The bush came free, the ropes slipped, the cowman slipped also and pitchforked over the ledge and man and cow landed in the straw, both winded, but luckily well supported.

Fitz, coming down the ladder, dropped the last few rungs and ran over to the cowman.

'I'm all right; just breathless. How's old Marny?' The man struggled to his feet, coming nose to nose with the cow, who was now standing, trying to make out where they had put her calf. She pinpointed the noise and lumbered off to the byre, determined to be with it.

Everyone followed.

The calf was lying in the straw. Marny, who now revealed herself was a nicely shaped little Friesian, her black and white markings like a jigsaw pattern all over her, was apparently very little the worse for her ordeal.

She bent to lick the calf, and silence descended blissfully on the farm. The cowman put the calf to suck; the first milk was the most important feed of all, as it was full of special substances that helped to give the calf protection against disease.

'Let us know if anything goes wrong,' Fitz said, a few minutes later, having cleaned his hands and face. His hair dripped onto his filthy shirt. Tamsin had already left.

'Now you see why we have Land Rovers,' Fitz said, leading the way to his battered old soft top. There was straw on the floor at the back, and Tim decided he would be wiser to sit on that; he'd make less mess.

The journey back was remarkably bumpy. Neither of them spoke. Tim was aware that he was ravenously hungry, and wondered what time it was. He seemed to have been at the farm for hours.

'I must say I've never had one like that before,' Fitz called back to him. 'Just as well you were here, as I think the calf would have died without you. There was no way we could get round to her other end and we dared not let go; she'd have been off the ledge. I'm black and blue all over.' He drew up outside the office door.

'Packed surgery,' Lisa said, coming out, 'and another calf in trouble; this one's lying down with colic and he wants someone out there fast. Who's doing surgery?'

'Tim can. Get cleaned up quick, and start on them. If you go you'll need a driver till you know the district. I can drive it blindfold.'

Tim raced into his cottage. There was no sign of Zia. The shower was much more useful than a bath. He shed his filthy clothes, showered and rubbed himself half dry, dressed rapidly, and raced down again to grab a slice of bread and chew it as he dashed over to the office. Zia was in her crate there asleep.

'She's fed, empty and been played with,' Lisa said. 'In you go. Busy morning.'

Tim hoped fervently that it would be an easy morning; he was more than half asleep and so hungry all he could think of was bacon and eggs, which wasn't going to help him at all.

All went well for the first half hour. He injected a cat that had been bitten by another and dressed the wound after cleaning it; the cat behaved fairly well; cats were never easy patients.

He treated a dog with a runny eye, re-assuring the owner, as the dog proved to have been sitting in a draught in the car the day before, with the window blowing on his face for nearly eight hours during a very long journey from the South. The dog, a gentle old labrador, licked his hand happily when he examined it.

A bitch in whelp came in to be checked over; he wasn't too happy about her condition; her coat was dull and she was lethargic, which the owner put down to her puppies, but Tim wasn't so sure. He suggested vitamins to add to her diet.

'I don't believe in that nonsense,' the owner said. 'In the wild, dogs live on other animals' droppings, on the guts of their kill, and only feed about once every fourth day. Most dogs are overfed. She has plenty of water, and I give her porridge; oats are very good for growing pups.'

'You can't feed her like that,' Tim said, appalled. 'She needs extra food; good protein, meat, fish, eggs, cheese; she's ravenously hungry with the pups inside her.'

'I've been breeding dogs all my life, young man, and I know what I'm doing. Next time I come, I want to see Mr. Fitzpatrick. He respects my methods; I have had several champions. They didn't come because I starved them.' She marched out. Lisa looked at him.

'I should've warned you,' she said. 'We don't know why she bothers to come, as she knows much better than any of us. She won't change; she's been like that for years. They'll be mangy little pups; and full of worms; and she'll sell them for a fancy price. You'll have to learn to smile and agree and say nothing. I don't know if she really believes her dogs are beautiful or if it's just sales talk. And she's never had a champion in her life, but we go along with the fiction for the sake of the dogs.

'That's going to be hard,' Tim said. 'That bitch is in a rotten condition. She might die whelping. Where's she kept?'

'In a draughty shed. Last time one of the bitches whelped, the owner didn't move her before the pups were born and the other two bitches killed all the babies; some people never learn. I only hope she doesn't do that again as the bitch fought to protect her babies and was very badly bitten. We had a dreadful time with her. Incidentally, any sick bitch from there comes into the hospital; I don't know why we bother as it isn't looked after when it goes back. Some people oughtn't to have dogs.'

Tim dealt with two cats with canker in the ears and provided a flea spray for a mongrel puppy that had been rescued by the R.S.P.C.A. He examined it. It was otherwise healthy, though badly underfed, and when the little animal was fit it had a home to go to where it would be appreciated, with an elderly lady who has just lost her life long companion and was willing to take on this.

'You'll love our last patient,' said Lisa, as she brought in the card. The door opened to let in a girl of about sixteen, balancing on crutches; beside her a big black and white mongrel, half collie, half something quite unidentifiable.

'Rass has cut his paw,' the girl said. 'Up, Rass.'

The dog, which was not on a lead, walked to the table, jumped up, and held up a badly bleeding paw for examination. Lisa helped the girl to the only chair in the room and leaned the crutches against the wall.

'It looks like glass,' Tim said. 'I'll give him an injection. Will you hold him, Lisa?'

'No need to hold Rass,' Lisa said. 'Meg's trained him to do everything for himself; he's better trained than a lot of guide dogs.'

The dog sat patiently, while the needle went in, and held his paw up while it was bathed and bandaged. He jumped down from the table when Meg told him he could, and went over to her, tugged at her pocket, brought out her purse, and took it over to Lisa.

'He knows the routine,' said Lisa.

Tim watched the two of them go through the door. Rass paused at the door, came back, sat in front of Tim and barked, before disappearing after his mistress.

'She sent him back to say "Thank You",' Lisa said. Tim, looking out of the window, saw the girl swinging herself expertly along the drive.

'Is she permanently crippled?' Tim asked.

'Yes. I don't know what's wrong; she had something wrong from birth. She spends all her spare time teaching Rass new things; he can go into the shops with the money, and bring out what she needs in a basket; he carries home the paper, and he watches over her, and if she falls, he barks till someone helps her; he fetches and carries for her at home. I don't know what she'll do when he's old and has to go. But he's only six; so that's well in the future.'

Tim sighed. It was always there. One of his patients that morning had been a very old dog almost at the end of his life. It was only a matter of weeks; his kidneys were failing and there was nothing anyone could do.

'With any luck, we'll have a short breather,' Tamsin said, coming into the office with a tray of coffee cups. 'Sugar, Tim?'

Tim nodded. He needed food.

'I'll go back to the cottage in a minute and get something to eat,' he said.

'No need,' said Lisa. 'I made sandwiches for both of you; Fitz won't have had a chance to have breakfast either, and here he is back by the look of it. He's a cat to neuter this morning and a cyst to take off from the leg of a red setter. She should be in by now; she's late.'

The Land Rover stopped outside the window and Fitz got out, and came into the room.

'Food, thank heavens,' he said. 'I nearly raided the hen run for raw eggs. Everything okay?'

'Mostly,' Tim said, through a mouthful of egg and cress and home baked brown bread. 'I upset a breeder with a rather out of condition bitch.'

'The woman from Crumbletop,' Lisa said. 'Mrs. Knowall.'

'That's a tough one; pity you had her your first day,' Fitz said. He paused to drink his coffee. 'We only have one or two like that. One or two who have ideas of their own about remedies; cold tea for eyes; and raspberry leaf tea for whelping bitches; you have to bear with them; and they usually agree to more modern methods if something is badly wrong.'

'I'm used to that,' Tim said, looking down at Zia who was stretching herself and waking. He removed the wire lid and lifted her out. 'My aunt is one of those.'

He went out, carrying the pup; maybe this time he could manage to get her outside before she puddled; he hadn't managed too well the day before. He put her down in the cottage garden and she trotted about and then squatted, looking up at him expectantly.

'Tell her she's a good girl,' Tamsin said, watching

over the fence. 'How else can she know? You'd better come to the dog club as soon as she's inoculated; and learn how to teach a dog. It isn't easy; till you know how and then like everything else, it's a piece of cake.'

'Do you go to the dog club?' Tim asked, after telling Zia she was a good puppy and feeling remarkably silly as he did so. She wagged her tail and ran over to him, and stood against his leg, begging for attention.

'I teach there,' Tamsin said, and walked off.

Tim didn't know what he'd done to annoy her; life did get complicated. He decided to spend a few minutes heel training Zia, and bent down to fasten her lead.

'Hey!' There was a yell from Lisa, and Tim turned his head.

'For pity's sake; the bullocks are in Mrs. Fitzpatrick's garden. Come on, quick.'

He grabbed Zia, dashed back into the surgery and put her into one of the cages. Zia began to howl, but at least she was safe.

Tim, glancing out of the window across the yard, was horrified to see that at least twenty bullocks were stampeding across the beautiful lawn, which was always smooth as a billiard table top. There was all the appearance of a rodeo as Fitz, shedding his operating gown, was trying to head them off from the flowerbeds, and Mrs. Fitzpatrick, her face grim and furious, was flapping her hands at them, and saying 'shoo' which seemed merely to anger them. Tails up, charging round, they headed for Fitz, who dodged them and turned the corner of the house.

'Lisa, for heaven's sake ring the farm; ring the police; ring for the Black Maria, ring for the fire engine! Tim, you're nearest. Go and dial 999, only hurry man. Don't argue. DO IT!'

It seemed to Tim a remarkably odd thing to do to get bullocks out of a garden but he went indoors and dialled. A bored voice said, 'Which service do you require, fire, police or ambulance?'

'Police,' Tim said, wondering what on earth the police would do. Maybe at this rate they would need an ambulance, as both Fitz and Lisa were in full flight. Mrs. Fitzpatrick appeared to have given up and gone indoors.

'Police. Can I help you?' a voice asked.

Tim, taking his eyes off the window, pulled himself together.

'There are about twenty bullocks in the vet's garden,' he said.

'Not again? I'll send up the Black Maria and can you ring the farm?'

'I'm new,' Tim said. 'I don't know the number. Everyone else is out trying to get rid of the bullocks.'

'Okay, I'll do it. What are they doing now?' the voice asked. 'Have you got a cine camera?' He chuckled.

All he needed was a funny policeman, Tim thought, as he put down the receiver, and went outside, only to be knocked right off his feet as one of the bullocks turned across the yard and came straight at him. He picked himself up as the bullock vanished into the shrubbery that Fitz had tried to keep safe from their heavy bodies and thundering hooves.

A car drove into the yard. Tim signalled frantically as the driver opened the door to let a collie dog out. A bullock raced in front of the car, and dog and bullock took off down the drive towards the road, the owner of the dog racing after them, shouting, 'Tippy, come here, do you hear me, Tippy! Here I say, here!'

Tim thrust his hand through his hair, took a deep breath and went off towards the shrubbery where Fitz, out of breath and also out of temper, was trying to herd the animals into some sort of order. None of them were co-operating. The flower beds and the lawn were a memory. One of the bullocks charged off towards the drive where another car had just arrived. The driver stopped and Tim yelled, 'Stay there! Whatever you do, don't get out!'

Seconds later, a large van drove in. The Black Maria. Were they going to arrest the bullocks? Charge them with being drunk and disorderly and put them all inside? Tim had visions of handcuffed bullocks sitting decorously in court waiting for the judge to pass sentence and wished his sense of the ridiculous would behave itself.

The policeman got out, followed by a very small brown faced man in old clothes and a cloth cap, accompanied by one of the oldest and greyest sheep dogs Tim had ever seen.

'Herd 'em, Fly,' the old man said. The police positioned themselves in every possible gap, and Fitz signalled to Tim to stand on a little path that led towards the back of his cottage. Lisa had already stationed herself beyond the corner of the surgery, and one of the policeman had shifted the two cars to block yet another gap.

The old sheep dog barked, and set himself at the heels of the furthermost bullock. Unbelievably the beasts herded, and with the dog chivvying them, went off towards the gap in the fence through which they had obviously come.

'Sorry about that, sir,' the old man said. 'New today, this lot, and skittish like. I'll get the fence mended at once. Better block it for now.'

Fitz stood and watched the beasts vanish down the field. Grim faced, he went over to an outhouse and brought out a piece of planking. Everyone gave a hand, and in no time at all they were nailing it in position, to provide a temporary barricade.

'Hope the beasts can't jump,' he said morosely, and

turned to face Mrs. Fitzpatrick who had emerged from the house.

She completely ignored everybody but the largest and most senior-looking policeman, who was in fact a constable and had been all his life. The sergeant behind him, who was slight and much younger, grinned at Tim as Mrs. Fitzpatrick advanced.

'I want to prosecute the farmer,' she said. 'Look at the damage to my garden; all my rare shrubs have been ruined; the lawn is ruined; the fence was broken down. Its criminal carelessness; if he can't keep his animals in order he ought not to be farming at all. See to it, officer.'

She went indoors. The sergeant grinned at Fitz.

'Want to prosecute?' he asked.

'Prosecute one of my best customers? Always pays his bills, and we do more than a thousand pounds of business with him every year. No way. We'll settle it over beer in the pub on market day. George is a fair man. He'll make up for it. Tomorrow he'll send a squad of his men over to relay the turf; not the first time and it won't be the last. Happens nearly every year when the new lot of bullocks come in.'

'We'll be off then. Someone down the lane lost a calf yesterday; we were searching for that when we got your message. Hope we've not got rustlers.'

'If it's a calf you're looking for, it's in our outhouse. Came in here last night looking remarkably weary and hungry. I forgot all about it in the fuss. Meant to ring you and tell you. She's okay now. Fed and watered and her owner owes us for an injection and for treating an injured hind leg; cut it on wire I reckon. Something scared her and she tried to jump.'

Tim watched the Black Maria drive away, the calf lying on sacks inside. A few minutes later an exhausted man, hatless and panting, arrived open-shirted, dragging a miserable looking collie dog on his tie.

'Haven't got a lead,' he explained to the air. 'Never thought I'd need it. Don't expect to find bullocks rushing around like mad things when you bring your dog for his booster.'

'Have you an appointment?' Fitz asked. His temper seemed to have suffered considerably during the past hour. He was covered in mud and had a large bruise on his chin where a hoof had kicked him. Tim had been kicked on the thigh and Lisa had fallen and cut her hand. They looked like wartime casualties and so did the garden.

The dog's owner had no appointment and was told to came back at surgery time and drove off. The second car proved to contain the butcher with meat for the dogs and for the deep freeze.

'I'm always scared I'll muddle them up,' Lisa said. 'Mrs. Fitzpatrick will get the dog meat and the dogs'll have fillet steak.' She laughed as she took the basket into the kitchen beyond the little hospital.

Tim picked Zia out of the cage and took her back into the office and shut her in her box. There was no time for her now. A woman came into the room, and smiled at him.

'I seem to have missed all the excitement. I've been sorting out the orders for medicines and supplies,' she said. 'I only work here in the mornings. I'm Sheila Grant, by the way. You're Tim; and I've met Zia. It's going to be fun to have a puppy around. Let her play for a bit. No-one comes in here. She won't disturb me and it'll do her good getting out and about. She needs to meet people and dogs, or she'll be timid with people and either be scared of other dogs, or go for them.'

Everyone seemed to be giving him advice on his puppy. No-one had looked at his diet sheet yet and suggested he altered that, but give them time. Tim lifted Zia out feeling a little irritated. Anyone would think he was back at school again being taught what to do and what not to do, instead of being out in the world on his own.

Fitz had cleaned himself remarkably fast and reappeared wearing his operating gown. Dressed in green from head to foot, he looked surprisingly unfamiliar. Tamsin was ready to help him.

'We're both trained animal nurses,' Lisa said. 'So can you dress that cat's leg again for me? The red setter's just coming in and I've got to shave her leg so that the cyst can be cut out. We're a bit late after all that carry on this morning.'

Tim went out of the room, and Zia raced after him. Sheila Grant called her, but she wanted Tim. He put her back in her bed and fastened the lid, and went into the hospital.

The cat watched him with baleful eyes as he opened the cage door. He picked him up and held him against his chest, soothing him till he purred. He wrapped the cat in a towel that lay on the counter by the sink, and took the bandage off the paw. The injury was raw. It had been torn by the under part of a speeding car that hadn't seen the cat in the dark and had left him lying, crying, and badly hurt, in the road. A cyclist had seen him and brought him in. No-one had claimed him.

'What will happen to him?' he asked Lisa as she brought the setter in, half doped by the sedative her owner had had to give her before she came in. The bitch lay quietly, while the shaving was done.

'I expect I'll have him; I have about five already,' Lisa said. 'Unless you want him; if you have him, you pay the bills!'

Tim re-bandaged the injury and the cat licked his hand with a rough tongue. He purred throatily as Tim scratched his head at the side of his ear.

He was aware of the ringing phone, and Sheila Grant's voice answering it in the office. He hoped it wasn't another emergency call. It would be difficult to find his way around without Tamsin and she was busy helping operate.

'It's your day off,' Lisa said. 'I'll give you a map and you can go shopping; I suggest you buy at least a fortnight's stores; we can get very tied up with emergencies. It's not too bad now; but wait till lambing begins. And the pigs here do the most peculiar things. So for that matter do the horses and the cats and the dogs and the parrots.'

Her voice was a soft monotone, and very difficult to hear. Tamsin came in and went off again with the red setter.

'Sorry about that,' Lisa said. 'The setter's very nervous; I was babbling to her rather than to you.'

'I think I'd better do some exploring, too,' Tim said. 'Or I'll be lost on the way to one of the farms, and never get there in time.'

'That's an idea,' Lisa said. 'I'll just go and get that map. You can go now, I should think. There's nothing to worry about.'

'There is,' Sheila Grant said. 'I had a call from the kennels over at Hollow End. One of the bitches is due to whelp in a few days and is acting very oddly; sounds like calcium deficiency. She's grabbed all the bones in the kennels and is going at them as if she were mad; trying to crunch them up.'

'Where is it?' Tim asked.

'I'm going home now; I'll come with you and show you, and you can drop me off on the way back. I walk here, and there's no one waiting for me,' Sheila said. She was outside and waiting before Tim had grabbed his bag.

The grey morning had given way to a bright blue day,

the sky clear, the leaves on the trees splendid patterns of tiger yellow and red and gold. One or two trees had lost their leaves and were stark against the sky. Green fields soared towards the sky as they drove towards the mountains. The peaks changed in the light, even as they drove.

The kennels were off the main road, down a winding narrow lane. Tim hoped they wouldn't meet another car; there was no room to pass and nothing to do but reverse back its whole length.

They turned again into a gateway, and found themselves in the yard of a beautiful modern house, behind it a stone barn, with a green door. The woman who came out was dark and slender, her brown hair pulled back into a pony tail held by a velvet ribbon.

'Thank goodness you were quick,' she said. 'I'll bring her out, away from the bones, as she's defending them against everyone but me. She's due the day after tomorrow; and she looks crazy.'

She ran down the little incline into the barn and appeared a few minutes later with an elegant but very much in whelp Afghan bitch, straining on the lead, her eyes completely wild. She carried a bone in her mouth, refusing to let go of it at any cost.

Tim took one look at her. The calcium injection was ready and he injected her quickly while the bitch's owner held her. She snarled, and, within seconds, the light in her eyes calmed and she dropped the bone and looked at it as if she'd never seen it before in her life and couldn't understand how it had got there.

'There's a girl, then,' her owner said and Tim held out a hand for the bitch to sniff. She stood calmly as he examined her.

'It's like magic always,' he said, watching the bitch return quietly to her kennels as if she'd never had a thing wrong with her.

'Come in and have coffee before you go,' the kennel owner said. Tim looked around for a notice saying which kennel it was and giving her name, and found it over the barn. *Pennyfarthing Kennels. Jean Loads*, the little notice said. He must find out names first, he thought; there was so much to remember. He looked inside, seeing a neat office corner, and a number of concrete kennels, with large enclosures beyond the bedding area where the dogs could roam. Two pretty little Afghan bitches, neither more than six months old, looked out at him.

They drank coffee in a peaceful room where the chestnut carpet was warm on the floor, with cream curtains and walls giving a restful air. The window table was banked with flowers of all kinds, growing in pots. A large black Persian cat lay at length on the rug, his tummy stretched to the fire. Sheila stroked it.

Beyond them the fields sloped to the hills; the hedges were bright with berries and a heron flew over, his back humped, his head sunk into his chest, his legs trailing behind him.

It was good to sit, briefly, and chat for a moment, but they couldn't stay long. Tim whistled as he drove back. It was a good end to the morning. The bitch would be fine now. And he'd been able to recognise the symptoms, though they were pretty obvious to anyone. He had liked the bitch's owner too; he compared her with Mrs. Knowall from Crumbletop, and was glad that he hadn't had to go out to that particular kennels.

He planned to spend the afternoon exploring with Zia. He'd hardly seen her at all all day; she wouldn't even know he was her owner at this rate.

All the same, it was a relief to know that she was being well looked after.

Time for lunch; time to go and explore; time to himself. He dropped Sheila at home, drove back to the surgery and pulled into the yard.

The high pitched whimper reached him before he turned off the engine. It sounded like Zia crying.

Tim ran.

Chapter 7.

Tim raced into the waiting room, and discovered the place had turned into a bedlam. Two small children sat on chairs, bawling at the tops of their voices, while a distraught woman held a small black bundle that dripped on to the floor. The noise came from the bundle, a distressed puppy crying that went on and on and on.

'She fell into a can of creosote,' Lisa shouted above the din. 'Mr. Fitzpatrick's operating on a dog that was in a car accident. Can you cope now, quickly?'

Tim took the puppy in his arms. He ran into the surgery, and filled the sink with warm water. Lisa and the puppy's owner were behind him. He added soapy liquid from the dispenser, felt the water, took a quantity of cotton wool and began to clean the puppy's eyes and mouth and ears. The puppy continued to cry.

'Will she die?' the owner asked.

Tim hadn't time to consider.

'She could. Look, take the children home and leave her with us; give us a ring about seven this evening. We'll know more by then and we'll keep her overnight.'

Lisa led the owner out, and presently her car drove off, the childrens' yells echoing on the wind.

'Will she be all right?' Lisa asked, watching the forlorn bundle as it slowly turned from a black mess into a small black and white puppy, with blotches on head and ears and legs, and a blotch of black over one eye giving it the look of a pirate.

'Depends whether she's swallowed it,' Tim said, lifting the crying animal out of the water, and handing it to Lisa who by then had a large towel. She wrapped the puppy up and talked to her softly as she dried her. She still stank of creosote.

'How did it happen?' Tim asked.

'Her husband was painting the fence and the children let the puppy out,' Lisa said. 'What shall we do with her?'

'Try filling her with milk,' Tim said. His second outfit that day had been ruined and he wondered how he was supposed to cope with his laundry. Everything he wore was stained black.

Lisa opened the small mouth.

'She's had it in her mouth; perhaps she didn't swallow,' she said hopefully and Tim, bending over the tiny animal, looked into its jaws.

'She's not in very good shape anyway,' he said, a moment later. 'She's far too thin, and needs feeding up. Looks like a collie crossed with a spaniel. Do you know the family?'

'They're new here,' Lisa was busy rubbing the little animal. 'What are you doing with her? Are you giving her any treatment or just warm milk? I'll make up some of the special puppy milk; it will be safer than anything else for her. I can't ring the owners; they aren't on the phone.'

'I'll give her an injection to counteract shock,' Tim said. 'She could probably do with vitamin injections too. Her treatment is going to be expensive. I suppose they can afford it?'

'With all those children? I don't know.' Lisa held the puppy while the needle went in. She cried out, and then lay quietly in her arms, exhausted by all that had happened to her.

'I'll put her by the Aga,' Lisa said.

She went out and Tim went into the office to look for Zia. She'd been put inside a large wire pen, rather like a child's play pen, and was surrounded by a number of unlikely toys. One of them was a large piece of drainpipe, made of plastic, which she carried over to him proudly, to show him.

'You're a nut,' he said, and lifted her out and fussed her.

The telephone bell rang.

Tim answered it.

'This is the vet speaking.' It was the first time he'd answered the phone; the first time he had called himself a vet and he almost missed the reply; he was so startled by the sudden thought that here he was after all those years of college, qualified and working. Tim Yorke, MRCVS.

He listened quietly, growing more and more bewildered by the voice at the other end.

'The dog keeps doing what. . .?'

The voice grew more excited.

'I think I had better see him at once,' Tim said. 'Bring him in. Have you a car?'

He rang off, and Lisa came back into the room.

'We thought Zia would be happier with more room to move. One of the breeders who we know well, and like for a change, saw her and brought this pen over for her. Let her have it back as soon as she's big enough; it'll keep her out of mischief and you can leave her with an easy mind if you don't want her in the car. What was the phone call?'

'A dog running round in circles, jumping over the chairs and making funny noises,' Tim said.

'What was the owner's name?'

'I forgot to ask. She's on her way over. She talks nineteen to the dozen; I was glad I wasn't a donkey.' Tim took off his stained jacket, and looked down at his trousers. 'What do I do about laundry?'

'We use the practice's washing machine; it's in one of the outhouses; I'll see to it for you this time. I'll call you when your patient comes; Mr Fitzpatrick wants you to have a look at the dog he's working on. Poor brute's in an awful mess. It had been dragged along by a car, and the flesh on its hind leg has been torn right away down to the bone; it's a major repair job.'

Tim looked down at his clothes.

'I'd better change out of these first,' he said.

He walked out of the room, and Lisa called after him.

'Why a donkey?'

'I wouldn't have any hind legs,' Tim called back, as he raced at top speed over to his cottage, and changed into yet another pair of trousers and a shirt. He would be able to double as a quick change artiste in the theatre at this rate, if he ever lost his job. He ran back. He never seemed to have time to walk.

The dog on the table was a mess. Tim looked down at him; the left side of his body had been flayed by being dragged on gravel; the huge wound gaped and though clean now, looked as if it would never heal. The leg had been neatly and beautifully worked on, so that though it was a very bad injury, it would work again, if only the wound healed. The bone showed clean and white.

'Why don't people learn not to let dogs wander?' Fitz said. He was angry; a tiny blood vessel in his forehead was beating. He hated working on a badly injured dog, knowing the suffering it was going to have from its future treatment.

'That's it, Tamsin. Put him in the warm. I can't do anything more now. Watch him as he comes round; I don't want him staggering about, or trying to tear at those dressings.'

'Shall I carry him?' Tim asked.

'I'm quite capable, thank you.' Tamsin said, and picked the dog up and took it out of the room.

'Our Tamsin believes in equality,' Fitz said. He took off his operating gown and cap, and removed his gloves. Lisa came in to clean up.

'How will he do?' she asked.

'He should be all right with careful nursing. He'll have to stay in. His owner runs a garage; no wife to look after the dog and he'll be too busy. I'm going home for tea. I've not had lunch yet. It's been a hell of a day.' He walked out, and Tim thought back; it seemed much more than a few hours since he'd been balanced precariously on a ledge with a calving cow.

He walked wearily out into the waiting room, which was lined with chairs and had pictures on the walls advertising various veterinary products. *Use No Season on your bitch. Feed your puppy Vitafit.*

There was an advertisement for the Dog Training School, and two more for boarding kennels; another recommended a cattery.

The twelve rules of conduct for Pet Owners were pinned up on the wall.

A car drove, far too fast, into the drive and braked savagely at the door. A small woman climbed out, wearing a startingly cut vivid blue dress that was far too short, a feathered hat put on sideways and carrying in her arms a large pekingese that appeared to be suffering from apoplexy.

He was a handsome cream coloured dog with a plumed tail.

The owner put him on the floor.

He staggered and fell.

'I can't think what's wrong with him,' she said. 'He's been doing that for nearly an hour; it wasn't so bad at first. It's getting worse and worse. I walked him in the fields at the end of the village; and he was feeding on something down there in one of the barns. He wouldn't come when I called. I don't know what on earth he's eaten. I hope he isn't going to die. . .'

'He's alive enough now; and it's not like any poison I've ever seen,' Tim said, trying to sound as if poisons cropped up daily. In fact he had never seen any cases of poisoning at all; the nearest to it was the creosote soaked puppy now drying himself in the warm corner of the hospital, a lamp above him and the Aga beside him.

Tim knelt by the dog.

He snarled feebly and snapped, but hadn't enough strength to do any harm.

'He never does that normally,' Lisa said. 'This is Leo; he's a very sensible animal; he behaves perfectly. We know him quite well; he must have picked something up.'

The dog was suddenly sick, bringing up a mass of what looked like potato.

Tim wrinkled his nose.

'He's drunk,' he said. 'That stuff stinks of alcohol.'

'Alcohol; in a barn?' The dog's owner looked blankly at Lisa. She appeared, on further acquaintance, to be a lot more sensible than her clothes suggested.

'I was rehearsing for a play,' she said. 'I totally forgot how I was dressed. Leo was all right up to about an hour and a half ago; we'd walked about half an hour before that.'

Tim was racking his brains for the antidote to alcoholic poisoning. It seemed to be something that had been left out by his lecturers.

'I think all Leo's going to have is a massive hangover,' he said. 'We'll give him something to make him sick again and then try him with coffee. Lisa, get some ice and wrap it up. Let's put it on his head and back.'

'You're sure he'll be all right?' The owner looked anxiously at Tim. She was younger than he had thought; when the light shone on the stage makeup he realised she had been made up to look like a much older woman.

He looked down at the dog. He could, this time, say with total honesty that Leo would be perfectly all right in a couple of days. He was beginning to feel horribly responsible. People expected him to work miracles; to wave a magic wand and effect a complete cure in moments and nobody could do that.

'Would you like to go back to rehearsal and let us work on Leo?' Lisa asked. 'You can pick him up tomorrow morning. He'll sleep it off. It's the first night tonight, isn't it?'

Leo's owner nodded.

'The real trouble is that Leo has a part in the play. It's near the end, when he's supposed to come on and bark. I suppose there isn't any chance. . .'

Tim looked at the dog and then looked at its owner. He'd heard of having to get drunken actors ready for the big night but this was ridiculous.

'We'll try,' Lisa said. 'We're coming to see you. We got tickets three weeks ago. If Leo's okay I'll bring him with me. If not, can you manage?'

'After a fashion. He always gets a big hand; and he's useful if it's going badly. You know what the village lads are like; I don't know why the vicar bothers. We get booed by them every year, and this year will be no different. It's a silly play.'

She went out and Lisa laughed.

'They put on a play at this time every year,' she said. 'The vicar's a nice man but he doesn't realise how dim we all are. Last year they did *The Rivals*; I don't think even the actors really understood their lines; and the year before it was *The Doll's House*; this year he's persuaded our village genius to write a play for them, and I believe it's very obscure; all about a man, and his better self and his worse self, and his shadow, and the situations they get into. He's got his eye on Sally, which is why he put Leo in. She does adore that dog.'

Tim took the pekingese into the surgery. Coffee and ice-bags seemed an odd treatment for a dog but he couldn't for the life of him think of anything else and when he looked up alcoholism in his textbook that was all the advice given. Leo was lying on his side, panting, obviously feeling as dreadful as a dog could feel. He lay there with an expression on his face reminding Tim of himself and his friends after a night's unwise indulgence.

'That's a mug's game, dog,' he said severely, and Fitz, coming in to the room looked amused.

'What's a mug's game?' He came over and looked at the little dog. 'Am I seeing things or is he as tight as an owl?'

'He's tight,' Tim said. 'He sicked up what looked like a mass of grain, or perhaps it was potato soaked in gravy.'

'Where had Sally been walking him?' Fitz asked.

'In the fields down the far end of the village,' said Lisa, coming in with the coffee and the ice bags. 'She said he went into a barn; it can only be one of Pritchard's barns, down there,'

'And Pritchard grows sugar beet,' Fitz said. 'That's not the first animal I've seen suffering that way; and it won't be the last. Better warn Sally not to walk him there unless he's on lead. People don't realise how many hazards there are in the countryside. Glass, barbed wire, mouldy sandwiches left by lazy picnickers; they cause us a lot of trouble, if dogs eat them. Last week we had a dog that had fallen into a quarry. The fence had rotted and trees were growing around it, and he went in after a rabbit. He broke his back.'

'Did he survive?' Tim asked.

'No, he died.' He patted Leo on the head. 'Never mind old fellow, you'll feel better by morning.'

'Sally wants him on stage tonight,' Lisa said.

'Oh glory, it's the first night, the great day of the village. I promised we'd go, but I can't make it. Anderson's Arab mare has started to foal and there's no way I'm leaving her without supervision, remembering the games we had with her last time. She's worth a large fortune – not that that makes any odds, but it makes him extra nervous. He's all his money invested in his horses. I promised I'd be there with him this time. Last time she nearly died of a misplaced foal. Better work on Leo with coffee if he's to do his bit for England tonight.'

Tim was dripping coffee into the dog's throat, using a syringe without a needle. Leo was breathing very fast. Tim hoped he'd been right; dogs as well as people could die of too much alcohol.

Lisa came back with yet another ice pack.

'I'd better take over. Your tea's in the office. Tamsin took Zia over into your garden for an hour this afternoon while we had a breathing space; she's had her tea as well, so no need to worry about her.'

Tim went into the office, and was greeted by Zia frantically as if he had been away for years. He felt a little that way himself. He fussed her, drank down the scalding tea, and grabbed three biscuits. At this rate he'd soon have ulcers, and he'd burned his mouth.

'You do remember it's your half day,' Fitz said, wandering in to the office, and looking out of the window at the trees. Sunlight behind them burnished the last late leaves.

Tim laughed. He had completely forgotten. He had been far too busy.

'Can I take the rest of the day off?' he asked. It was too late to go shopping but it would be heaven to have time to think; time for unpacking; time for Zia. He seemed to have been moving at top speed ever since he'd arrived and it was impossible to believe he'd only come the day before.

'I'll ring you if there's an emergency,' Fitz said. 'In any case I'm afraid you'll have to cover for me while I'm over at Anderson's. We've had trouble with that mare on and off for the last two months. She's one of the most beautiful creatures I've seen; the sort that would make a man commit any crime in the world to own. You must come over and see the stud some time. Most people have never seen horses like them in their lives.'

Tim went back to Leo and took him through into the little hospital room where the big cat with the injured leg purred when he saw him. It was lonely in his cage and he loved people coming to and fro. He rubbed himself against the bars and Tim tickled his forehead.

'One of our regulars is in surgery tonight,' Lisa said, coming in to the room. 'Tony is the biggest Tom I've ever seen and one of the worst fighters. He regards the whole village as his territory so he's kept busy, and so are his owners. I can't think why they don't neuter him. It would be much cheaper than spending a fortune patching him up after fights. He's a real battle scarred old warrior and age doesn't seem to stop him either. He must be nearly eleven years old and fighting fit is the only way to describe him.'

Leo had fallen asleep on the rug in the corner. Lisa bent over him. He opened his eyes and wagged his tail.

'He should be okay. He'll have to be kept quiet though and even then he might not manage to stagger on stage,' Tim said. 'Let me know how it goes.'

He collected Zia and her crate from the office and went across to his cottage. The next few hours were busy. By the time he had finished, the wardrobe and chest were full of his clothes and other possessions; the picture of a racehorse, perfect in every detail, that he'd always coveted, had pride of place on the sitting room wall. His father had bought it for him when he finally passed his exams. There was the solemn owl his sister had given him on his sixteenth birthday to remind him of the baby owl he had looked after until it was ready for flight. Ambrose had been a difficult pet, needing a very odd diet of mice which were surprisingly hard to come by. It was a relief when he decided he was old enough to live in the wild again. Seven puppies romped round a verse on another picture that had been given him as a going away present by his mother.

It was about dogs and ended with the lines:

Besides which many men seem logs,
I know no finer thing than dogs.

Tim thought of Leo lying in a drunken sleep and laughed. Zia woke and whimpered. He took her into the garden, and watched her nose around the ground. There was a tiny hummock. She backed away from it, growling. Tim was puzzled until he remembered the molehill and the earth that had been thrown in her face. She obviously thought this would do the same thing.

She came over to him when he flicked his fingers and leaned against his leg. She was a woolly furry bear of a pup, her brilliant eyes looking up at him adoringly from just below his knee. She was going to be a big animal; even now she took up a large part of the hearth and the crate would very soon be too small for her.

Night had come while he worked. The moon hung low over the trees, a glowing orange ball across which fine clouds chased endlessly, brushed by a whistling wind that would strengthen later to a gale. It whined in the trees and the pup crouched against him, shivering.

'It's only the wind, you nut,' Tim said, rubbing her head. 'Let's go in.'

There had been a nip in the air and the warm room was a welcome haven. Everyone in this area had open fires; logs blazed in the hearth and the firelight was friendly, the dancing shadows reminding Tim of days spent with his grandmother, sitting at her knee while she read to him.

He prepared Zia's last meal, and then went back to arranging his possessions. He had a shelf full of books that he hoped might be useful; books on managing mares and foals; on breeding pigs; on managing a dairy herd; books on sheep husbandry and breeds of sheep. He had noticed that most around here were Suffolks; a breed he liked, with their black faces and black legs and neat bodies and thick plush wool, like a baby's furry toy.

The cattle were mostly black and white Friesian but he had seen a Jersey herd, beautiful pale caramel coloured animals with large soft eyes, grazing in a field by a river; the scene idyllic enough for a television commercial.

There was still his last case to unpack.

He sat back on his heels looking at memories of his boyhood. He had relented and packed one copy of *Treasure Island*. Oh, Aunt Dora, he thought. A patterned black and red jar with a cork lid that was full of rubber bands. They came in useful for a lot of things. His wall clock, beautifully carved, that his uncle had given him after a visit to Switzerland.

A tiny figure of Paddington the Bear with his straw hat and wellies that Trish had sent him as a mascot before his final exams. He put him up on the mantelpiece, a bright patch of blue and red, with his label, *Please look after this bear, thank you.* Tim grinned. It was just like Trish with her sticking out pigtails and the brace on her teeth to give him something so silly.

There was the mug with his name on it that Aunt Dora had made for his birthday long ago. *Timothy Ivan Neil Yorke* for all to see.

His Uncle Ted, who was an artist, had lettered a card for him; it was beautifully done, with tiny horses galloping round the edge, interpersed with kittens in all kinds of attitudes; and a busily scratching dog in several poses. The words were those of a Celtic blessing.

Deep peace of the Running Wave to you.
Deep peace of the Flowing Air to you.
Deep peace of the Quiet Earth to you.

Deep peace of the Shining Star to you.
Deep peace of the Sun of Peace to you.

He looked at them when he was tired; he could imagine the endlessly moving sea and waves breaking on smooth sand; the wind on the hills; the warm summer earth, and lying on the ground, looking up through the green leaves of trees at the blue sky; the bright stars at night, in a dark sky, of total peace.

It was very soothing after a hectic day and it would be even more soothing now, as if every day was like today, life was certainly going to be hectic.

He drew the curtains and shut out the dark. Zia slept on. Lisa had given him half a pasty and made a salad when she had made her own tea; he must repay her somehow, but it was good to heat soup, and drink it slowly, with crusty new bread; to eat the pasty and salad, and watch the firelight dance on the walls of his own home; his own dog lying asleep in her bed, twitching slightly as she dreamed. He made himself a cup of coffee, and sat by the fire to drink it, eating Lisa's fruit cake.

The fire crackled invitingly as he put on more logs.

He thought back over the cases he'd seen; all those years of study and so far he'd done the oddest things, a drunken dog; a puppy that fell in creosote; a calf delivered on a cliff.

No-one had told him that working as a vet would be like this.

The little clock that his uncle had given him ticked away the minutes with a busy noise. Zia woke and he took her outside. He played with her, throwing a small ball made of paper which she brought back to him again and again, standing in front of him, eyes expectant, asking him to throw it, please, again and again.

He found himself yawning more and more, and made

a last drink, took Zia out for a last time and then put her in her bed, where she curled up, already at home.

He was so tired when he finally fell into bed, that he slept at once, only to dream that he was standing on a ledge far too narrow for him, trying to put ice packs on the back of a very drunk cow while Tamsin poured coffee into it down a trombone, wearing a very short blue dress and a hat that was bright with peacock's feathers.

He fell off the ledge and woke with a jump and grinned to himself, and fell asleep again, this time to dream of nothing and only wake when the pealing telephone shrilled its din into the darkness.

Chapter 8.

Tim woke muzzily. It must be the middle of the night. He picked up the phone, switched on the light and looked at the clock. Five in the morning. Lisa's voice spoke into his ear.

'Sorry, Tim. There's a horse with colic at one of the farms; the farmer's been up with him all night but feels that he must have a vet to see him at once; he's been walking him, but it isn't working and last time he went down he could hardly get up.'

'I'll be down,' Tim said. 'How do I get there?'

'Tamsin will be over; Fitz said she was to chauffeur you to emergencies to save time; no use getting lost and losing an animal. I'll have coffee for you and if you leave the key with me, I'll see to Zia.'

He dressed in a daze, dragging on trousers and pull-over over his pyjamas, hoping he'd have time to take them off later. Zia woke and fussed, but he had no time; he was outside drinking down the coffee as Tamsin drove into the yard.

'Hurry,' she said, and he handed Lisa the cup and was in and off, driving through the darkness, the lights picking up hedges, a startled cow's head looking over the fence; and a field where the sheep ran as the powerful lights scythed across them.

Colic. He was racking his brains to remember all he could in case it wasn't straightforward. Colic could be a killer and he didn't want to lose his patient, but had the farmer delayed too long?

It could be due to wrong feeding; or poisoning; or internal damage; or stones in the kidney; or pregnancy, if she were in foal.

'Mare or gelding?' he asked.

'Gelding, so it's not due to foaling,' Tamsin said, thought reading. She had been a veterinary nurse for six years and knew a great deal. She would have liked to have been a vet but she had a father crippled by a road accident and a semi-invalid mother to look after; and no-one could afford to pay for help in her family. Maybe one day she would go off to college and qualify but that was a long way in the future.

They turned into a rutted lane.

'We'll have to walk the last part,' Tamsin said. She grabbed her wellingtons; Tim's were always part of his farm visiting gear and were on him already. Field or stable, neither were places in which you wore shoes.

The gelding was a big black Shire, a well made animal that was in great distress. He was blowing through his nostrils, breathing noisily, his eyes glared wildly and he kept turning his head and staring at his side as if he could identify the pain and remove it that way.

'Is he rolling?' Tim asked.

The farmer was a small dark man, his face grey with weariness, the morning stubble dark against his skin. His clothes were covered in bits of straw. He soothed the horse, stroked its neck and spoke to it, but it was blind to everything but its own pain.

'Not now; he's crouching sometimes; he started last evening, just after bringing him in. I ought to have rung before, but it seemed to be going off and then it started again.' He moved swiftly as the horse stamped a forefoot and turned rapidly, presenting its rump to them.

Tim was already at work on the horse; feeling his body; hoping desperately that this was not a complicated case needing operation; he had no idea how he could cope with that alone; he was suddenly sweating as much as the horse; repeating over to himself the causes of colic as if they were a prayer that could help him; as indeed they might, he thought. Maybe Aunt Dora would have a herbal remedy for this.

Tamsin joined him, carrying the drench he intended to try first; if that succeeded they could all relax.

'Have you drenched him?' he asked.

'I've not given him a thing,' the farmer said. 'He got loose yesterday; he got into my far field and I found him at the potato clumps; think he might have eaten potatoes and given himself a belly ache.'

'Could be.' Tim was too busy to do more than answer briefly. The horse reared suddenly and the liquid he was pouring into it poured down Tim's shirt. Tamsin took over; she was deft with her hands and gentle and kept up a soothing 'there, there, there,' as she worked. It looked so easy when she did it.

Tim wished he had more experience. Theories were all very well until you were faced with the animal in reality and this fellow was enormous; one swipe from those hefty hooves. . .wow. That wasn't a funny thought.

No temperature.

The horse pawed the ground again.

'Walk him when he's in pain and let him rest when it eases,' Tim said. 'He's getting very tired.'

The farmer nodded. He was removing the horse blanket which was soaked with sweat. Tamsin began at once to lay straw over the animal's back, while the farmer brought another blanket and fastened it firmly.

Tim watched as the horse was walked slowly round the yard, which was lit now by the headlights from their car. Tamsin stood beside him.

'I think he's easing,' she said.

Tim nodded.

Tamsin looked at her watch.

'Are you here alone, Mr. Ellis?' she asked.

The old man nodded.

'Can I go and cook you some breakfast? Did you eat

last night?' She nodded in her turn as he shook his head. 'I'll cook a meal and then I'll walk His Lordship while you eat.'

'Make enough for both of you then,' the old man said. 'Time's getting on and you'll be starting work as soon as you leave here.'

He looked at the horse. The strained look on its face was going, and the breathing seemed fractionally easier.

'I think it's working,' he said.

'Time will tell; if it's only overeating, he should clear in a few more hours,' Tim said. 'He's a fine beast.'

'One of the best; I bred him myself, but had to sell the rest of my horses; life's getting too expensive for small farmers; keep goes up and I hadn't enough hay last winter and had to buy in in the hungry gap.'

He leaned against the wall, looking momentarily sicker than his horse.

'Life's not much these days, mister. All work and no play and no money spare for pleasures; that's why I waited; it'll take time to pay your bill and Mr. Fitzpatrick doesn't like slow payers.' He sighed and turned his head as Tamsin came across the yard.

'Go and eat,' she said. 'And rest before you start the day's work or your horse won't have a master.' She took the rope and began to lead the horse round the yard again. He followed her quietly.

'She's a grand lass,' the old man said, his mouth full of bacon and fried bread. 'Pity about her parents. The old man's a devil since his accident; leads her and her mother a hell of a life. He was a good chap till the car took away his legs; he was knocked down one night by a hit-and-run driver; they never got him, more's the pity. Left Fred in a very bad way. That's life, I suppose; not been the same for me since the old girl died. Heart attack a few years back.. There's not much point to living alone and if His Lordship has to go I'll be finished; he's all I've got that I care about now. Except for my sheepdog; Bess is a rare clever animal.'

It was time to get back; time to start the day's work, without a moment to spare, and Tim wondered if he would even have time to wash and change. Tamsin drove fast, in total silence.

He got soap in his eyes washing; drank coffee that he didn't want because Lisa had made it for him, not knowing he had already fed. Zia was in her pen and her whole body wagged in ecstacy when she saw him. At this rate she wouldn't be his dog; she'd belong to everybody.

'Many waiting?' he asked.

'It's packed. Yesterday's patients are okay. I dressed Buster's leg; Leo managed to walk on stage without looking as if he would fall on his side every minute and as he didn't have a speaking part he did it well; he got a terrific ovation. There's one thing though. . .' she was taking cards out of the filing cabinet, matching them to her list of clients, and putting them in order. 'You know the pup that drank creosote?'

'She isn't dead?' Tim asked, catching his breath; suppose he'd done the wrong thing.

'No. They rang up to say they don't want her back; can we find another home for her. She's dirty and a nuisance.'

'Why the hell do people take on animals they don't want,' Tim said in fury, not thinking about Zia at all.

'It was a present from a neighbour; her bitch had eleven puppies and she couldn't find homes for them so she gave them to friends. I don't think she has many friends left. The R.S.P.C.A. have one of them; this is the second I've heard of going begging.'

Tim walked into the surgery and put on his white coat. He felt irritated and exhausted; he'd been up since dawn on his second day and it was hard to stifle his yawns.

He smiled at the woman who came in, dragging a reluctant fox terrier that sat firmly on its bottom and skidded along the floor, holding desperately to the lead with both paws.

'He hates vets,' the owner said brightly., 'You're a silly boy, aren't you, Soo soo?'

'What seems to be the matter?' Tim asked, hoping she would be brief; Lisa seemed to have about twenty cards already and another car had just drawn up outside the window; it looked like a town car park from his viewpoint.

'His anal glands need squeezing; he's sucking his paw and skidding on his tail all the time and I know he hasn't got worms because he's been tested,' she said.

That was easy enough, apart from the fact that the dog objected, and as Tim squeezed the glands under his tail, turned his head and planted his teeth firmly into Tim's wrist.

'He doesn't mean it,' the owner said, displaying her own hands, which were both bitten in several places. 'He's a very high spirited little thing.'

Tim was speechless. He watched Tamsin take the owner outside, and marked up the card, before holding his wrist under the tap.

'I only hope he hasn't got rabies,' he said crossly. 'What on earth makes people think a dog should bite as matter of course? Doesn't she ever try and stop it?'

'You can go off dogs if you work here long enough,' Lisa said. 'The terrier's gone, having piddled against a chair leg, so the dog next door did too, and if we don't watch we'll have a flood out there. Once one does it they all start.'

It was going to be one of those days.

Tim bandaged the next dog's mouth, having by now also bandaged his own wrist, as he had no desire to add another bite to that. The owner protested; her dog wouldn't bite, but Tim wasn't taking any chances; he had already been up for four and half hours and treated an enormous horse; that was enough excitement for one day without adding another bite to the fun.

He treated a cat that had been bitten by a rat; it scratched him.

'All we need is a snake, and a snake bite,' Tim said morosely. Ten o'clock had come and gone and there were still several people left in surgery.

He watched the next dog walk in, in disbelief. He was an enormous German Shepherd, walking beside his owner, off lead.

'Samson, sit,' she said and the dog sat.

'Samson had a lump removed from his back ten days ago,' Lisa said. 'He's come to have the stitches out.'

'Is it easier sitting or standing?' the owner asked.

'Standing; will you hold him?'

'No need. Samson, staaand.' She patted his head and he looked up at her, adoration in his eyes. That was what Tim wanted to see from Zia.

'Stay, there's a good fellow,' the owner said. She was a tiny blonde woman who must, Tim thought, be well on the way to fifty.

He discovered later she was well over sixty. Her voice was soft and calm and the dog obeyed it instantly. He removed the stitches, wishing all dogs were as well trained.

'Tim has a standard poodle puppy,' Tamsin said, coming into the room. 'Tim, this is Mary Hayes, she's one of our top performers at the dog club. I've told them you and Zia will be coming, so you can show our patients how a dog should behave.'

Tim looked at her blankly.

'Tamsin's like that,' Mary said. 'You ought to see her little collie; she's taught him all kinds of things and he's every bit as well trained as Samson. It'll be lovely to have a standard poodle join the class. The Americans use them for work much more than we do; it's a pity not to, as they are such intelligent animals. Come on then Samson, thank Mr. Yorke,' she said, and the big dog walked over to Tim, sat and solemnly held out his paw.

Tim laughed and shook it.

He watched owner and dog walk quietly out through the waiting room. The dog sat while the car hatchback was opened, and when told, jumped into the vehicle and lay down.

'That was an R.S.P.C.A. rescue case,' Tamsin said, bringing in a small kitten in her arms. She stroked its head and it opened a minute mouth and mewed at her. It was draggled and dirty and had a badly injured leg. 'The dog was vicious, out of control and the owner swapped him for a guitar to someone who turned him in to the R.S.P.C.A. after a week.'

Tim thought of the beautiful perfectly controlled dog that had just gone out, and took the kitten.

'Whose is this?' he asked.

'Nobody's. One of the men working on the drainage scheme down the road found it in a plastic bag in the trench. It had bitten a hole in the bag or it would be dead; can you make it comfortable for now and then it looks to me as if it needs operating on. Poor little devil; it's been in water as well. The man will take it home with him if we can get it fit.'

Tim looked at it; some people would have put it down but it had survived a major ordeal and was very much alive.

He gave it an injection and Tamsin took it out to the hospital to dry it and make it comfortable. The gash was nasty but Tim thought that it would only need cleaning and dressing and perhaps a couple of stitches.

He was relieved to find that the last five dogs were

quiet and sensible and only needed their boosters.

The door closed behind the last client, and he walked into the office and sank down on the window seat. Zia squealed at him and beat her tail against the pen sides.

'It isn't the dogs that have a dog's life,' Tim said with feeling. Lisa had made sandwiches for them all; he would have to operate in a few minutes, but right now he had to rest; he was so tired he felt as if he had been working for weeks.

'It's easier when you get used to it,' Lisa said. 'And everything's happened since you came; it's not always quite as bad as this.'

A car drove fast into the yard, braked to a standstill and a young man leaped out. He ran to the back of the vehicle and lifted out a dog wrapped in a blanket. Tamsin ran.

'Accident,' Lisa said, recognising the situation at once. 'Action stations, come on Tim. By the way there's a letter for you; did they call you TINY at college?'

Tim glanced at the envelope.

His mother!

T.I.N. Yorke MRCVS.

He had hoped the nickname would never be known here, but from Lisa's grin as she measured his height with her eyes, it was now part of him that he would never live down.

A moment later he'd forgotten everything as he looked at the dog. It was a beautiful pointer, but the car that had run over it had done major damage. Sheila took the owner to comfort him with a cup of tea, and Tim and Tamsin set to work.

Within seconds he had forgotten everything but the need for speed to save the dog's life, and he was fervently thankful for Tamsin's expertise as everything was ready for him before he realised he needed it.

The minutes ticked by; the anaesthetic machine

poured its life saving substance into the dog; outside a train rumbled in the distance, and Fitz returned in his Land Rover, looked briefly into the operating room and went away to talk to the owner.

'He'll be all right,' Tim said, an hour later, walking into the office where the dog's owner sat white faced and desperately anxious. 'We'll keep him in for nursing here for a few days; he's been lucky; he's a mess at the moment but nothing vital's been harmed; he'll be as good as new in a few months, but he'll need careful handling and exercising, as he has a broken pelvis.'

Lisa took the owner to the hospital to see the dog; he lay quiet, still under the anaesthetic, but cleaned and with his injuries dressed and the worst of them bandaged. The worst damage had been on his left foreleg. That would take months to heal.

Tim, looking down at his first major case, felt sudden total satisfaction. This was what he had trained for. This was what it was all about. The owner, though worried, was smiling, as he stooped to stroke the dog.

The black cat was watching as if he understood.

Then the puppy that had swallowed creosote came across the floor, a tiny bundle of black and white, now clean, though her mouth was still sore. She sat in front of Tim, between his shoes, and gazed up at this enormous man. She put both paws against Tim's leg.

'Two dogs would be as easy as one, wouldn't they?' Tim said, as Tamsin turned to look at him.

Her face broke into a delighted smile.

'You'll do,' she said, and Tim felt as if he had at last come home.

DOUBLE TROUBLE! by Joyce Stranger 75p
0 552 52132 9 Carousel

There was a yelp from the last dog, and it stopped searching to lick frenziedly at its paw. The dog was high on the hill and the rocks there were steep and jagged. The handler running to his dog yelled back.

'Glass! He's cut an artery!'

Tim raced towards them. Up over the rocks, panting and gasping for breath, his feet sliding from under him. He was whipping the cord from his anorak as he ran. He would need to tourniquet if he could – if only the cut weren't in the wrong place. The handler was kneeling beside his dog, pressing his hand over the wound. Blood spurted all around him. . .

Tim's new life as a vet was full of ups and downs; some were happy, some were sad, some were just infuriating – but at times like these his worries were lost in the desperate struggle to help an animal in need. This was what he was trained for – this was truly where he wanted to be. . .

An exciting sequel to VET ON CALL by the same author.

JASON by Joyce Stranger 60p
0 552 52113 2 Carousel

Nobody wanted the pup. He was born to a pedigree golden labrador bitch and his father was a giant mastiff. The owner of the bitch was furious and got rid of Jason as quickly as he could.

His first master didn't really like him very much – he only wanted him as a guard dog, and one day Jason ran away – looking, although he did not know it, for a master whom he could love. And when he found Duncan Grant, a boy who was as lonely as Jason, they were bound together in an instant and enduring friendship.

But even then Jason's troubles were not over, for Duncan's father would not let his son keep the dog. . .

KHAZAN by Joyce Stranger 75p
0 552 11014 0 Corgi

In all Debbie's bleak existence, nothing had happened – until the day the horse was washed up on the Cornish coast. The young girl who saved his life found her own miraculously transformed. Suddenly she found new friends to help her in her desperate fight to keep him. For Khazan captured everyone's imagination. A King among horses, born to race. . .

A DOG CALLED GELERT by Joyce Stranger 75p
0 552 09399 8 Corgi

Gelert was a handsome, fully grown Alsatian. He was lean, strong and sleek. He had wise warm brown eyes and he walked to heel, close against Barrie's leg, never taking his eyes off his master, ready to obey. Gelert meant more to Barrie than anything else in the world. But Gelert was just a figment in Barrie's imagination.

For Barrie Evans, who lived in a tall, grey block of flats in the city where no pets were allowed, where reality was being teased and bullied all day at school for being short-sighted and Welsh, Gelert was the only friend he had.

So Barrie ran away. He ran to escape the filthy noisy city, to find the countryside again. And suddenly he heard something that stopped him in his tracks. A soft crying coming from inside a derelict building. And there, gently feeling his way inside, Barrie found a dirty, hungry and beaten puppy. . .

If you would like to receive a newsletter telling you about our new children's books, fill in the coupon with your name and address and send it to:

Gillian Osband,
Transworld Publishers Ltd,
Century House,
61–63 Uxbridge Road, Ealing,
London, W5 5SA

Name ....

Address ....

....

CHILDREN'S NEWSLETTER

All the books on the previous pages are available at your bookshop or can be ordered direct from Transworld Publishers Ltd., Cash Sales Dept. P.O. Box 11, Falmouth, Cornwall.

Please send full name and address together with cheque or postal order—no currency, and allow 40p per book to cover postage and packing (plus 18p each for additional copies).